[Advance praise for *Hard Knox*]

"You want funny? You've come to the right place. This is Jack Knox, heir apparent to Stephen Leacock, at his high-flying best. Witty, wry, breezy and wholly original, Knox wields his humour with a deft hand and a sure grip. Canada needs more Knox!"

WILL FERGUSON
three-time winner of the Leacock Medal for Humour

"There are a few key secrets to a happy life in Victoria—avoiding downtown when the cruise ships are in, knowing exactly how late you can get to the ferry terminal, and reading Jack Knox."

MARK LEIREN-YOUNG
author of *The Killer Whale Who Changed the World*
and the Leacock Medal–winning *Never Shoot a Stampede Queen*

"Jack Knox isn't just a words guy, although that's important. He's also a guy with an eye (okay, two) for the inane and a mind geared to asking, 'What if?' And that's where the words come in, because he takes all that stuff, bounces it off the wall, and cranks out observations always amusing, mostly spot-on, and often fall-down funny. Plus, he doesn't think proper grammar is grandpa's prissy wife. Ain't a lot of that left."

JIM TAYLOR
sports columnist (ret.), author of *And to Think I Got in Free!*
Highlights from Fifty Years on the Sports Beat

"Jack Knox is one funny guy, but don't let the word play and wit fool you. He's a sharp and savvy observer of the Vancouver Island scene, and his affection for the place and its people shines through in his writing."

JODY PATERSON
journalist and communications strategist

"*Hard Knox* may cause dizziness, light-headedness, coughing fits, and sore ribs from laughing. If conditions persist after 224 pages, consult your bookseller about a sequel."

TOM HAWTHORN
journalist and author of *Deadlines: Obits of Memorable British Columbians*

HARD KNOX

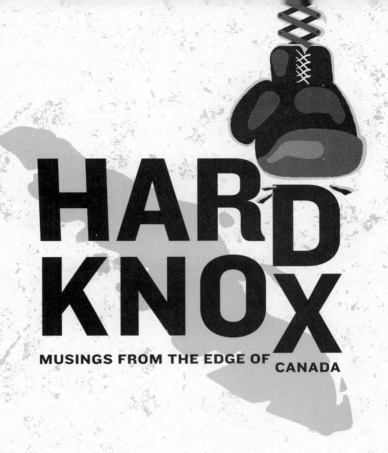

HARD KNOX

MUSINGS FROM THE EDGE OF CANADA

JACK KNOX

FOREWORD BY
IAN FERGUSON

VICTORIA • VANCOUVER • CALGARY

Heritage House Publishing Company Ltd.
heritagehouse.ca

CATALOGUING INFORMATION AVAILABLE FROM LIBRARY AND ARCHIVES CANADA

978-1-77203-149-2 (pbk)
978-1-77203-150-8 (epub)
978-1-77203-151-5 (epdf)

Copyediting by Grace Yaginuma
Proofread by Kari Magnuson
Cover and interior book design by Jacqui Thomas
Cover images: portrait of Jack Knox based on photo by Darren Stone; boxing glove illustration by Meriel Jane Waissman/iStockphoto.com
Interior illustrations by Jacqui Thomas

The interior of this book was produced on 100% post-consumer recycled paper, processed chlorine free and printed with vegetable-based inks.

We acknowledge the financial support of the Government of Canada through the Canada Book Fund (CBF) and the Canada Council for the Arts, and the Province of British Columbia through the British Columbia Arts Council and the Book Publishing Tax Credit.

20 19 18 17 16 1 2 3 4 5

Printed in Canada

To Lucille,
who has stuck with me for more than thirty years.
I question her judgement.

FOREWORD

Jack Knox owes me money. Not for this foreword, which I am both honoured and privileged to provide (a phrase I am lifting directly from every hockey interview ever: "Dougie, you scored thirteen goals in the third period, nine of them while balancing a Fabergé egg on a spoon; this truly has to be one of the greatest individual efforts in the history of the sport." "You know, it takes twenty guys working together and we had a pretty good game and it's an honour and a privilege to be part of this team."). Besides, Canadian publishers can barely afford advances for their authors, let alone pay some guy for writing the part of the book that even the most dedicated readers will skim over. No, the reason Jack Knox owes me money is because I like to start my day with a cup of coffee and the *Times Colonist* newspaper, which employs Jack Knox as a columnist. So he's a columnist for the *Colonist*. He's also one of the funniest writers in Canada, and hands down the funniest column writer in the entire country. Which is not intended as faint praise, because we have some very funny folks here in the Great White North, and many of them have the job of providing humorous articles for newspapers or magazines. But—as funny as others might be—none of them is funnier than Jack Knox.

This is why he owes me money. When I lurch out of bed in the morning and stagger bleary-eyed, in my pajama bottoms and faded "World's Greatest Uncle" T-shirt (which I won fair and square, mainly by a rather liberal interpretation of what constitutes healthy food and a proper bedtime) out onto my front porch, fumbling for the newspaper, I am both looking forward to and apprehensive about how the rest of the start of my day will unfold. Once I glance at the headlines ("World's Shortest Bridge Still Over Budget and Still Not Finished," "New Proposal for Sewage Treatment Plant Presented in Interpretive Dance,"

"Mayor's Plan to Allow Backyard Chicken Coops Applauded by Raccoon and Fox Lobby"), I immediately turn to page three, to read Jack Knox. That's the part I mentioned I look forward to. The part I said I was apprehensive about is when what he's written makes me laugh so hard I snort coffee all over my kitchen table. And my newspaper, of course, which is why I believe he owes me money. They don't give the *Times Colonist* away for free (though that may soon be part of the business model), and there's been many a day that started with my copy soaked with Folgers (I'm not a coffee gourmet, viewing it strictly as a caffeine-delivery system, which makes living in a city with a barista on every block a tad ironic), which means I'm not going to be able to read my horoscope ("Today will be a good day to use a J-Cloth.") or, even worse, the comics. I get a bit grumpy when I can't keep up with *The Other Coast* because the pages are too wet to turn, and coffee stains often ruin the punchline. This is why I moved to Victoria. I used to read Jack's columns online, and I got tired of spraying coffee all over my laptop keyboard. It was cheaper to relocate.

Here's the thing. Jack Knox isn't just a humorist. He's got a real job. He's a journalist. He also writes incisive and detailed feature articles and incredibly moving and thoughtful human-interest stories. So he's not just funny. But when he is funny, he's laugh-out-loud funny. And he's funny on a deadline. I get asked to write the odd (sometimes very odd) column. Occasionally *Maclean's* will call up wondering if I might do a piece on the best Canadian jokes, or the *Globe and Mail* will request something amusing about hockey, or the *National Post* will ask me to comment on some political gaffe. I'm always happy to oblige, and I'm always astonished by the amount of time and effort it takes to come up with 750 or so words about whatever subject they've suggested. Well, to be honest, coming up with 750 or so words isn't actually all that hard. Coming up with 750 or so *funny* words? That's hard. If the actor Edmund Kean (or possibly the actor Edmund Gwenn . . . and really, what are the odds these are two different people?) actually said on his deathbed, "Dying is easy, comedy is hard," then comedy on a deadline is really, really hard. Jack Knox makes it look easy.

In the interest of full disclosure, I should point out that I consider Jack Knox to be a friend, though I was a fan of his before we ever met, and I've been telling him for years that he should collect his funniest columns and get it published, you know, in book form. I'm not the only one who's been after him to do this, so I don't take any credit for what you're holding in your hands (assuming you are holding a copy of *Hard Knox*, that is), but I have been referring to him as "Future Leacock Medal Winner Jack Knox" since he first told me that the fine folks at Heritage House had jumped at the opportunity to publish him. And, of course, I jumped at the chance to write this foreword, simply so I could say that I've been "between the covers" with Jack Knox, as they say in the book world. Although, again, in the interest of full disclosure, we were both excerpted in *The Penguin Anthology of Canadian Humour*, but I got selected through sheer nepotism (my brother Will Ferguson was the editor), and Jack was chosen strictly through merit.

This book should come with a "laugh-or-double-your-money-back" guarantee, or a "hurting from laughing" warning. And, although the full title is *Hard Knox: Musings from the Edge of Canada*, you don't have to be a resident of Victoria or a citizen of Vancouver Island (these can be mutually exclusive) to enjoy it. This is a book that will make all of Canada laugh. All of which is to say, you have made an excellent purchase (unless you shoplifted your copy, which is probably not a good thing to do, though Jack would still get his royalties, and, you know what? I'll leave situational ethics to the professionals, like politicians and tel-evangelists and philosophy professors and such). I commend you for your fine choice and excellent taste.

One thing, though: you probably shouldn't read this book while drinking coffee.

—Ian Ferguson

Ian Ferguson won the Stephen Leacock Medal for Humour for his book *Village of the Small Houses* and is the co-author (with his brother Will Ferguson) of the runaway bestseller *How To Be a Canadian: Even If You Already Are One*, which was shortlisted for the Leacock and won the Libris Award for non-fiction. His follow-up, *Being Canadian: Your Guide to the Best* Country in the World*, will be published just in time to help celebrate Canada's 150th anniversary.

INTRODUCTION

Sheltering from the rain in Sooke one day, I found a pair of handwritten advertisements tacked side by side on a coffee shop bulletin board.

"Firewood," read the first. "Douglas fir, dry, split, delivered, $90 a cord."

Right next to it, under the heading Souls Reclaimed, was a flyer posted by a woman who, for a certain consideration, would put you in touch with whomever you happened to be in previous incarnations.

This was utter nonsense, of course. Everyone knows you can't get a cord of dry, split fir for ninety bucks.

But lost your soul? If you have moved to the West Coast, you have moved to the right place.

Better still if you have washed up on Vancouver Island.

For if British Columbia marches to the beat of a different drummer, Vancouver Island dances to a band that no one else can hear at all. It's where people go when they don't fit in anywhere else.

Just look at the map, the way it's tucked down in the lower left-hand corner of Canada, like a stray sock forgotten at the back of the drawer. People don't end up here by accident. They come because it's the end of the road, because it's as far from normal (or Toronto) as you can get without drowning. Call it the Island of Misfit Toys, the last refuge of the disconnected and the disaffected.

It is a function of history. This is not the Maritimes, populated by United Empire Loyalists. This is not Quebec or Ontario, where the roots run hundreds of years deep. This is not the Prairies, where farmers are tied to the soil. This is British Columbia, where just about everybody's grandparents came from somewhere else, searching for something else.

They came in waves: Spanish sailors, Scottish explorers, English remittance men, Chinese labourers, and California gold miners chasing a dream. The most restless migrated to Vancouver Island: Finnish utopians, British cultists, American draft dodgers, sixties longhairs, and refugees from Bush 2.0 and Trumpism, finding a home in the forests that provide so much of the province's wealth.

By reputation British Columbians are lumberjacks and space cadets, hewers of wood and fryers of brain cells. Vancouver Island? More free spirits than a distillery tour. It's where the snowbound part of Canada shovels its flakes.

We provide other Canadians with endless hours of entertainment, constantly delighting them with everything from tree-hugging hippies and self-hugging hipsters to naked yoga, nine-dollar coffee drinks, $1.2 million bungalows, and our pioneering experimentation with the warm-weather hockey riot.

That's not even mentioning the Ringling Bros. Circus that breaks out whenever snow hits the West Coast. There's nothing that brings a smile to the frostbitten lips of those living in Violated Livestock, Saskatchewan, like the sight of panicked Victorians going into earthquake/tsunami/Armageddon mode at the first hint of a wintry dusting.

But that's okay. It just means we on the Coast are fulfilling our purpose in life: to provide comic relief for the real Canada, the one with the block heater cords, square tires, and sheets of cardboard shoved between the radiator and the grille of the car.

For we all have our roles to play in the great Canadian drama, our stereotypes to confirm.

Albertans are the rednecks, a province of hard-eyed, hard-working conservatives who chew tobacco, drink rye, and spit out hippies.

Saskatchewan and Manitoba are like Alberta, only with more humour and (usually) less money. Think *Corner Gas*. We can't understand why Alberta isn't more like Saskatchewan, home to the sunniest Canadians this side of Newfoundland. Saskatchewanians endure year after year of bad crops, bad weather, and the Roughriders, yet remain resolutely, unreasonably optimistic. They are like Jimmy Hoffa's dog, sitting at the end of the driveway, waiting for him to come home.

Ontario? With a population of 14 million, it has more people than Sweden, Belgium, or Greece. Yet in stereotype they're all clones, like Agent Smith in *The Matrix*, identical Toronto careerists decked out in corporate climbing gear (suit, tie, underwear) as they fight their way up the ladder in the Centre of the Universe.

Quebec is the well-dressed sibling, hipper and haughtier than the rest of us. We suddenly become conscious of our Kirkland-brand lumpishness when Quebec sweeps into the room with a scarf flung around its $1,600 Harry Rosen jacket.

The Maritimes? Lobster traps and ceilidhs, except in tiny PEI, which has an economy built entirely on potatoes, *Anne of Green Gables*, and bridge tolls.

Newfoundland is the merry rowdyman, full of screech, bereft of cod.

As for the North, it's melting. Bummer.

British Columbia? Here's how Matthew Engel of Britain's *Guardian* newspaper once described it: "A beautiful land of vast spaces and mild climate; of mountain, river and forest; a land of great wealth but a tradition of compassion; of racial diversity but far more tolerance than strife."

Why, thank you, Matthew.

But while the province is "definitely one of God's better ideas," Engel continued, "its politics are vicious, corrupt, polarized and rather charmingly wacko."

Damn straight, Matthew, and proud of it. Not for us the bloodless, dollar-driven banality of those bland, grey, solemn suits who shuttle between Parliament Hill, Queen's Park, Bay Street, and corporate Calgary. We like our politicians the way we like our veggie burgers—hot, greasy, nutty, salty, and half-baked. Canada's other premiers appear on *The Nation's Business*. Some of ours could have gone on *Cops*. A shady Louisiana governor once declared that he wouldn't get chucked from office "unless found in bed with a live boy or a dead girl." In BC he'd go up eight points in the polls. But that's just politics.

This is the province where you can shoot heroin in broad daylight in the streets of Vancouver but struggle to buy a beer in a grocery store, where nobody thinks it odd that the Sunshine Coast gets forty inches of rain a year, and where workers moan about having to dress up for Casual Friday.

Vancouver Island is like BC on crack. Only in Victoria can you smoke dope outside city hall with little fear of consequence, yet risk public flogging by the Tobacco Police if caught cracking open a pack of Player's Light. Yes, Victoria, where your bicycle costs more than your car, where the Yellow Pages have fourteen listings for aromatherapy but just two for snowmobiles, where medical marijuana dispensaries outnumber Tim Hortons by a ratio of four to one.

Then there's the rest of the Island, where the communities fall in two categories: those without a Starbucks are either a "beleaguered former mill town" or a "struggling former fishing village," while anywhere with a golf course and more than six Alberta licence plates is known as an "affluent retirement haven." (Sometimes we get confused and write "beleaguered retirement haven.")

Except here's the thing: while the stereotypes might be rooted in reality, there's more to us than just that. If you're thinking about moving here, even if you're only planning a visit, there are things you need to know—the brutal truth about Islanders, their history, their way of life, the way they look at the world.

To really know us, you have to spend time here. That's the purpose of this book, to give you that experience vicariously. That's why this series of essays/incoherent ramblings is ordered in the way it is, as something of a drunken stumble through a year in Victoria, the City of Gardens. Some of the pieces are rants, some are just slices of ordinary life. Added, where appropriate, are a few of my columns from the *Times Colonist* newspaper, plunked in whole when they emphasize the point I want to make.

Maybe these lessons from the School of Hard Knox will give you the urge to join us here in Dysfunction-by-the-Sea—or maybe they'll make you grateful that we're safely on the far side of the moat. Write this off as an island of lost souls if you will. We prefer to think of them as reclaimed.

Okay, let's start by pushing the elephant in the room out the door. Let's talk about what really separates the Wet Coast from the rest of Canada...

THE WEATHER
(AND OTHER CLASSIC HUMOUR)

It was no good. I couldn't go on. The snow was too deep, the ascent too high, the unrelenting, deafening gale sapping every last ounce of strength. Frostbitten fingers had long lost the ability to grip an ice axe.

As wind-driven ice crystals whipped my cheeks—pellets fired from the mountain gods' own shotgun—I turned to my climbing companion, lifted his ear flap, shouted to be heard: "You go for the summit! I'll make my way down to base camp!"

"What do you mean, 'summit'?" the letter carrier replied. "I'm heading for your mailbox. We're only going up your driveway."

Yes, but it's a very steep driveway, or at least one with a slight incline, the kind of slope you never notice until it snows, which it never does in Victoria, except for every winter.

Oh, go ahead, rest of Canada, have a good laugh. Laugh at Vancouver Island brought to its knees by the kind of weather that Winnipeggers equate with Labour Day. Laugh at Victoria,

where the city's three-stage snowfall response plan consists of (1) demanding Justin Trudeau do something, (2) calling in sick, and (3) fainting.

For this, we accept, is the West Coast's role in the great national theatre: to provide a little winter amusement, a bit of comic relief, for our frostbitten and parka-wrapped compatriots. The rest of Canada enjoys a BC snowfall the way the Brits enjoy watching Princess Anne fall off a horse.

As mentioned in the introduction to this book (what, you skipped the intro?), we all have a stereotype to play in this production: Albertans are rednecks, Torontonians self-obsessed, and Newfies fun-loving. Montrealers are hipper than you in either official language. Saskatchewanianites, or whatever, are salt of the earth.

Us? We're total wimps when it comes to winter, each floating flake sending us ducking and flinching like Lee Trevino in a lightning storm. And Lord but it makes the rest of the country feel good to watch us dig the Westfalia out of the ditch.

For this is the truth: if the US can be split between red states and blue, Canada also exists in two solitudes. No, not French and English, but Snow and No Snow. On the West Coast live people who think a fleece vest is a winter coat and minus thirty is the sale price. East of the Fraser Valley—beyond Hope, as it were—exists another race whose knuckles are permanently scarred from bashing them across the grille of the car as they uncouple the frozen extension cord from the block heater cord.

This latter group speaks an arcane language dotted with curious references to "square tires," "gas line antifreeze," and "the smell of burning cat hair when the engine finally starts." Canadian Tire sells 60 percent of its block heaters on the Prairies, where it has just 15 percent of its stores.

This Snow/No Snow split is also known as the Starbucks/ Tim Hortons divide. A *Canada.com* editor named William Wolfe-Wylie once mapped out an analysis of where the two chains have coffee shops.

"Tim Hortons owns Eastern Canada and the highways between major cities," he found. "Starbucks owns the urban core." Vancouver was the only major metro area that, from downtown to suburbia, tilted toward the latter. (In Hollywood, they joke that you can always tell if a movie has been filmed in Vancouver: there's a Starbucks in every shot.)

Overall, Timmy's dominated the Canadian coffeescape. "While Starbucks runs just under 1,200 Canadian locations, Tim Hortons has more than triple that number," Wolfe-Wylie wrote.

But a quick look at the Yellow Pages showed that, like Vancouver, Greater Victoria ran completely opposite to the national trend, with three times as many Starbucks as Tims.

This is an important distinction, as it shows the West Coast differs not only in climate, but culture. In national mythology, Tim Hortons is for real Canadians: snowmobile boots, chainsaws, hockey sticks. Sheets of cardboard jammed in front of the radiator of the pickup truck in winter, beer around the campfire in the summer, followed by a shot of DEET.

Starbucks is for people with pink hands, expensive sunglasses, and Lululemon gear. They know what quinoa and couscous are, eat tofu on purpose. Starbucks customers have their heads buried in their laptops and iPads; Tim Hortons customers just talk to each other. Timmy's people build pipelines, Starbucks people protest against them.

Still, nothing separates Canadians like the weather. Every summer, West Coasters have to endure endless meteorological war stories from visitors who swagger in with terrifying tales of ice storms, whiteouts, and murderous, softball-sized hail. ("Peeled the paint right off the pickup! Brained your uncle so hard he can't count past fourteen no more!")

The implication is clear: they are real, weather-hardened Canadians, while we are a collection of limp-wristed, soft, pink quasi-Canucks whose reaction to the first falling flakes is to close the schools and bolt for home. Just a hint of white in the sky and the entire city of Vancouver goes to voice mail. By 3 p.m. it looks like France in 1940, the commuter routes to Burnaby and Surrey choked with ox carts and refugees fleeing the advancing horror.

Ditto for Victoria, though at least we have an ace to play.

"But what about the Blizzard of '96?" we squeak in protest. "It was the third-highest one-day urban snowfall in Canadian history!"

Ah, yes, the Blizzard of '96, which Victorians speak of in the same grim, hushed tones that Canadian First World War vets used when recalling the carnage of Passchendaele.

Over December 28 and 29, 1996, a total of 124 centimetres (that's forty-nine inches, for those who still don't speak Trudeau) fell on the city. That was in addition to the snow that had been falling since Boxing Day. The city was completely paralyzed for days on end. It didn't help that (a) we only had a handful of snowplows in the entire region, and (b) the thirteen municipalities that make up Dysfunction-by-the-Sea couldn't coordinate which streets to clear.

Anyhow, Victorians still wear this catastrophe like some pathetic red badge of courage, as if the idea of a whole week of snow would send shivers down the already-frozen spines of our cold-blooded countrymen.

This may be why in places like Broken Snowshoe, Manitoba, there are people who pray, pray, pray that the next time the West Coast is on the television, the words *Tsunami Relief Fund* are strung across the bottom of the screen.

Not that we Lotus Landers do much to discourage this resentment. Indeed, we encourage it.

Take, for example, the annual Victoria Flower Count, a late-winter event in which residents are urged to tally and record the number of blossoms they find.

The flower count is all in fun, of course, a tongue-in-cheek, light-hearted reminder by Tourism Victoria to other Canadians that while they—and here I paraphrase—are trapped in a never-ending, frozen, soul-sucking, Ingmar Bergman film festival nightmare of icy roads, stings-like-razors sleet, gunmetal skies, barren trees, and frostbitten extremities, followed by a snow melt that promises nothing more than six months' worth of suddenly thawed dog leavings lurking in grey-brown slush, we here in God's country are basking in a paradise where the blossoms arrive before your T4 slip, and the grass grows green in winter and brown in summer, as opposed to the other way around.

As part of this good-natured exchange, Tourism Victoria sends fresh-cut daffodils to media outlets across Canada and the northern US, where media members good-naturedly hurl them into garbage cans.

(True story: In the late 1970s some bright spark at BC Ferries thought it would be a super idea to drop daffodils on downtown Calgary from an airplane as a springtime tourism promotion. Alas, it was minus ten in Calgary that day, and the flowers, being 90 percent water, froze into icy spears as they plunged. They shattered as they hit the pavement, spreading panic and yellow-green shards of biodegradable shrapnel. Fortunately, no one was hurt, though the *Calgary Herald* did publish a cartoon featuring a daffodil-dazed pedestrian. Some believe this story was the inspiration for *WKRP in Cincinnati*'s "As God is my witness, I thought turkeys could fly" episode.)

We who live in the City of Gardens know that the flower count—also known as the Festival of Bite Me, Toronto—isn't actually based on real science (if it were, Stephen Harper wouldn't have let us talk about it). We tend to fib a bit in tallying the number of blooms.

In 2012, for example, Victoria's sixth-coldest February on record led into a flower count week during which The Weather Network screen constantly flashed those big, red, here-comes-Armageddon Environment Canada warnings: snow, howling wind, locusts. Yet we still somehow managed to claim 2 billion blossoms.

Never mind. What really mattered was the rest of the country got the message that we are different, that while they sit gripping their ice-cold Timbits, tears turning to ice halfway down their frostbitten cheeks, here in the lower left-hand corner of the country floats a paradisiacal Shangri-La that has more in common with Grand Cayman than the Great White North.

In fact, we have even succeeded in convincing ourselves that what we enjoy is the Mildest Climate in Canada. We keep telling ourselves this, again and again, while doing the backstroke down Government Street during the raging sou'easters that slam us each fall, sending giant cedars crashing on our roofs and *Perfect*

Storm-ing fishboats to the bottom of the chuck. (A few years ago, the climate was so mild that a mildly hurricane-strength storm toppled stones that had stood as native grave markers on Race Rocks for fifteen hundred years. I'm not making that up.)

"At least we don't get as much precipitation as Vancouver," Victorians like to boast, and they're right. Weather records show the capital only sees rain twice a year: on the August long weekend, and then again from September to July, non-stop. Saying it rains less in Victoria than Vancouver is like saying Stalin was more huggable than Hitler—it's all relative.

This last year has been particularly brutal. December brought a series of violent storms broken only by the occasional state of emergency. Santa Claus bailed out of the Christmas parade and was replaced by Captain High Liner. The cast of Up with People was placed on suicide watch. Inverted, broken umbrellas blew down the rain-soaked streets like tumbleweeds. (Though, real Victorians don't own umbrellas, as to do so would be an admission that yes, it is going to rain. It's like buying a single bed: better to remain in denial.) The storm drains backed up; like Keith Richards in the 1980s, the ground got to the point where it just couldn't soak up any more, needed a little time to dry out.

Astrid Braunschmidt, the CTV meteorologist, gave up on using a teleprompter for her forecasts, just cracked open the Bible and began reading straight from the book of Revelation: wind, flood, fire, pestilence, and a plague of toads.

Flipping the channel, I got something similar from Ed Bain at CHEK: "It will rain tomorrow, and the next day, and the next. It will keep on raining until the last vestiges of life drain from my sodden soul and wash down the storm sewer. Then it will rain on my grave." Ed is a cheery guy.

It was soon after that, while driving down-Island—grey highway merging into grey mist into leaden sky, rain streaming like sweat off a television evangelist—it occurred to me that for a place that's supposed to be paradise, Vancouver Island can be flat-out gloomy. I mean sodden, miserable, turn-all-the-lights-on-at-3-p.m. dreary. In the rest of Canada, *Fifty Shades of Grey* was a bestseller; here, it's the colours of the rainbow.

It wouldn't be so bad if the rest of the world took our weather seriously.

If this were Montreal, they would call out the army. If it were Toronto, CBC would have a docudrama in the works, with Ryan Reynolds playing the captain of the Maple Leafs. In Florida, all the CNN reporters would be fighting over who got to do the live look-at-me-getting-blown-around-in-the-hurricane thing, the one where they finally decide to go inside after a flying No Parking sign just misses Anderson Cooper but takes the arm off a cameraman before embedding itself, kung fu–style, in a UPS truck.

But Victoria? Other Canadians ask us, "What's wrong?" and we say, "It's raining really hard," and then they roll their eyes and ask if we need a crisis-response team or just some dry rolling papers.

Meanwhile, we have endured week after week of nuclear-winter winds and firehose rain and are sloshing around in the sodden remains of Venice-by-the-Pacific, here on what yet another travel magazine has just dubbed "the best island in North America." (So what was Island No. 2—Alcatraz? Baffin? That one from *Jurassic Park*?)

Wobbly yet defiant—or maybe just punchy—we urge Mother Nature to bring it on: Is that it? Is that the best you can do? Give us another shot. And another one after that, but don't forget the lightning this time. And the locusts. Where the hell are the locusts? If you're going to go all Biblical on us, do it right: A plague of locusts. Wailing. Gnashing of teeth. Bailing of basements. And some boils. Don't forget the boils, just like Job got.

So it begins to snow, which, as I have already explained, it never does on Vancouver Island, except for every winter.

As I write this, this contradiction is piling up outside. Worse, it's not melting.

Islanders normally deal with snow the same way we deal with a jealous spouse on the doorstep: close the drapes and ignore it, and eventually it will go away. Not this time. This time it has not only stayed, but called in friends with baseball bats.

And that howling wind! I put the dog out to pee, and it phoned half an hour later from Seattle, asking for a ride home.

The cat looks like it was patted backwards. BC Hydro has suffered more blackouts than the aforementioned Mr. Richards on a Jack Daniel's binge.

And cold? It has been minus eight degrees Celsius, or minus eighteen with the wind chill—not that this impresses anyone who lives beyond Hope. The rest of Canada doesn't believe in wind chill. It's like saying a player stands six foot eight with his skates on, when he's really only six foot five.

Want to feel wind? Try Saskatchewan in January. I used to live in Regina. Go to the west side of town—you could find Big Mac containers that had blown in from Edmonton. Go to the east— you could smell the stench of rotting principles wafting in from Ottawa. If we drag wind chill into the equation, Reginawanianites, or whatever, will just think we're soft as Charmin.

This is not entirely true. We are what we like to think of as Island Strong. For example, our periodic earthquakes don't faze us at all. This being Vancouver Island, half the people don't even notice when the house starts shaking, figure it's just the brown acid from Woodstock coming back to haunt them. Back in 2001, we had a quake where a ceiling panel fell and busted in two over my reporter friend Judy Lavoie's head, right there in the *Times Colonist* newsroom. She was like George Chuvalo fighting Muhammad Ali: it buckled her knees, but she wouldn't go down, just kept plugging away on her story. Earthquake, shmearthquake. I'd like to see a *Regina Leader-Post* reporter take a shot like that and still hit deadline. But I digress.

Earthquakes are something we have grown to accept, if not actually relish, on the West Coast. The little ones, the occasional temblors that rattle the teacups and send emergency-preparedness kits flying off the store shelves the next day, are accepted with only a mild amount of sphincter-tightening.

As for the Big One—or, to be precise, the threat of the Big One —well, it's the only thing that gives us any Canadian street cred.

We are warned, repeatedly, that we will soon be clobbered by the kind of shaker that will result in a dust-smudged Ian Hanomansing doing CBC stand-ups in the rubble where the legislature steps used to be. Note that much of Port Alberni was swamped by a tsunami from the Alaska quake of 1964, and that in the year 1700, the entire coast from mid-Vancouver Island to northern California was devastated with a massive mega-thrust earthquake. Scientists say another monster shake is imminent.

The mere threat of this catastrophe, this ticking time bomb at our feet, tends to make visitors from the rest of the country nervous, which is something we like to milk for all it's worth. "I thought about buying green bananas," we tell our flatland friends, "but..."

Then we shrug with a fatalistic insouciance, safe in the knowledge that when scientists talk of an "imminent" earthquake, they're looking at a calendar, not a watch. So, yes, we're comfortable living with the seismological sword hanging over our heads.

At least we don't have to shovel it, not like real Canadians.

This is the most plagiarized piece I ever wrote. (By which I mean I was the one who was ripped off, not the other way around. Had I done the plagiarizing, I would have called it "research.")

Since it first appeared in 2005, various forms of this column have popped up on the Internet. I once received a copy, one in which the names of people and places had been changed, from a reader who said, "You should try writing something like this." On another occasion, a truncated version was published under another writer's name by a competing newspaper.

While the individuals named in the column might have changed in the past decade or so, it—alas—remains an accurate reflection of the way Islanders react to snow.

Also, the Times Colonist *did once publish a headline reading "Mainland Cut Off from Civilization."*

THE ATTACK OF THE
KILLER SNOWFLAKES

Chronology of a crisis, Vancouver Island–style.

5:35 p.m. Environment Canada predicts two to five centimetres of snow will fall on Victoria within a twenty-four-hour period. Weatherman Ed Bain reads the forecast on air, turns white, and faints.

5:40 p.m. Victoria mayor Alan Lowe issues immediate appeal for federal assistance. Prime Minister Paul Martin promises to send in the army.

8:45 p.m. Victorians begin queuing at tire stores, leaving vehicles in line overnight to be first served in morning.

10:15 p.m. It turns out BC's last army base, CFB Chilliwack, closed in 1997. Martin promises to send in navy instead.

10:20 p.m. Navy announces deployment to San Diego and Hawaii for "security reasons." Conservative leader Stephen Harper suggests prime minister call Quebec advertising agencies to shovel the snow, "since that's where the Liberals are spending all our money anyway."

6:22 a.m. Temperature plunges. Word spreads that Saanich man found ice on windshield. Curious neighbours gather to watch him scrape it off with credit card. One motorist, a former Albertan, claims use of mysterious "defrost" switch on dashboard can aid in process.

8:15 a.m. Terrified downtown skateboarders lose toques to menacing mob of balding, middle-aged men. "We tried to run," they say, "but those stupid baggy-assed pants made us fall down."

9:30 a.m. Hardware stores sell both of their snow shovels. Islanders begin cobbling together implements made from kayak paddles, umbrellas, plywood, cookie sheets, and Boogie Boards.

10:00 a.m. Golfers switch to orange balls. Beacon Hill Park cricket players, anxious not to repeat the ugly "snow blower incident" of the Blizzard of '96, switch to orange uniforms.

Noon Word of impending West Coast snowfall tops newscasts across Canada. Saskatoon hospitals report epidemic of sprained wrists related to viewers high-fiving one another.

1:20 p.m. Elementary schools call in grief counsellors. Grief counsellors refuse to go, citing lack of snow tires.

2:30 p.m. Rush hour begins an hour early as office workers come down with mysterious illness and bolt for home. Usual traffic snarl is compounded by large number of four-wheel drives abandoned by side of road.

2:50 p.m. Airplanes are grounded and ferries docked. No way to travel between Island and rest of the world. Newspaper headline: "Mainland Cut Off from Civilization."

3:22 p.m. Prime Minister Martin announces Canada's rapid-response team, DART, can be on the ground within six months.

"We can't leave Victoria to deal with 225 centimetres of snow on its own," he tells Lowe.

"Um, that's two to five centimetres, not two-two-five," replies the mayor.

The prime minister hangs up.

3:33 p.m. Provincial government responds to crisis by installing slot machines in homeless shelters.

3:45 p.m. Builders of new arena announce weather-related delays will push completion date back to July 2008.

4:10 p.m. At behest of Provincial Emergency Program, authorities begin adding Prozac to drinking water.

4:15 p.m. Fears of food shortage lead to alarming scenes of violence and looting. Grocery shoppers riot across the city, except in Oak Bay, where residents hire caterers to do rioting for them.

4:30 p.m. Bracing for the arrival of snow, the city is gripped by an eerie stillness reminiscent of Baghdad on the eve of the invasion. Searchlights comb darkening sky for first sign of precipitation.

4:48 p.m. Panic ripples across region as word comes in that first flakes have fallen on Malahat. False alarm. "Flakes" turn out to be nothing more than anthrax spores released by terrorists. An uneasy calm returns to city.

5:40 p.m. Weatherman Bain, shaking uncontrollably, tells viewers that snow warning has been extended. This weather pattern could go on for days. Mercury plummets to Calgary-in-August levels. Martial law is declared. Victoria-area politicians announce plans to establish emergency command centre aboard HMCS *Regina* once it reaches Oahu.

It's Valentine's Day in Canada's Most Romantic City...

CHICKTORIA

In 1862, women were so scarce in Victoria that a pair of "bride ships" were sent from Britain to address the imbalance.

"The girls are coming! The girls are coming!" shouted the *Daily Colonist* as the SS *Tynemouth* drew near, and the whole town shut down when the vessel finally arrived with sixty potential wives aboard.

A few months later, close to a thousand men crowded the docks when the second ship, the *Robert Lowe* (the Rob Lowe? Really?) pulled in with thirty-six marriageable women.

Pause to reflect on that scene as you ponder life in modern-day Chicktoria, a.k.a. the Most Romantic City in Canada, a.k.a. the City That Fell in Love with Itself.

For this is what you must know if you are contemplating moving to Victoria: the bride ships are no longer needed. The teeter-totter has tilted the other way. Eligible men are in shorter supply than Doritos at a 4/20 rally—and that has skewed their view.

To say the pendulum has swung is like saying the Donner Party was a bit peckish. The last census showed that of the 313,000 Victorians over the age of fifteen, there were seventy-seven thousand unattached women but just sixty-two thousand unattached men. That's a gender disparity of fifteen thousand.

The gap might explain why any Victoria male who is (a) single, (b) breathing, (c) not currently addicted or incarcerated, and (d) has his own car and/or teeth is referred to as "a catch."

The shortage only accentuates the appeal of a group of men who are, collectively, already pretty much top of the line when it comes to smouldering sex appeal. Just ask us—we'll tell you. Frankly, it's surprising that women don't swoon like fainting goats upon encountering the typical Victoria guy, whether he be the Standard Model (Tilley hat/fleece vest over paunch/fanny pack/Lord Baden-Powell baggy Boy Scout shorts/grey beard/yellow teeth/black dress socks with brown sandals), UFC Fighter Wannabe (camo sweatpants/Ed Hardy T-shirt/flaming-skull neck tattoo/ninety-day roadside driving ban), or Middle-Aged Cyclist in Overtaxed Spandex (no description required).

It's amazing that women manage to suppress what must be an almost unbearable desire for the Clooney clones walking, or perhaps waddling, in their midst. Time and again I am humbled by the restraint shown by those who manage to mask their yearning. ("That will be two twenty-five," said the coffee shop cashier, speaking in code. "Good Lord, you people are insatiable," I replied.)

Some women disagree with this assessment, arguing that the gender inequity has left Victoria's men with an overinflated view of themselves. This applies not only to unattached males, but to those with partners. It's not as though the average husband/boyfriend has exactly been cast in God's image, not unless God leaves His underwear on the floor, buys an ironing board for Valentine's Day, openly ogles the hot teachers at His kids' school, and barks out, "Who stepped on the duck?" after breaking wind.

To which the men of Victoria quickly counter by playing their trump card: we must be awesome, because—for the fourth year in a row—Amazon.ca has declared Victoria to be Canada's Most Romantic City.

That's right, baby, we're number one.

The online retailer bases its annual rankings on the sales of romance novels, relationship books, heartstring-pulling movies, and recordings by the likes of Michael Bublé, Dean Martin, and Luther Vandross.

In fact, Victoria topped every single category in 2016. The most purchased movie was *The Hundred-Foot Journey* (which I thought was about the women's room lineup at a Bublé concert but turned out to be a rom-com), while the top book was part of the Fifty Shades of Grey series (which I thought was about West Coast weather).

It's not just Amazon putting us atop a list, either. Not long ago, online retailer PinkCherry.com bestowed upon us the title of Canada's Sexiest City, based on the per capita sales of lingerie, adult novelties, and sex toys (Victoria: Home of the Newly Wed and the Nearly Dead Batteries). In 2015, second place went to the suburb of Colwood (bedroom community indeed!), while even the mid-Island community of Parksville—which, with a median age of 58.2, is the oldest city in Canada—cracked the top twenty-five.

Further proof that the BC capital is something special was provided in 2014 by *USA Today*, which included Victoria as the only Canadian entry among its Ten Best Romantic Winter Getaways in North America.

"Mountains meeting the sea is always a sublime setting for romance," read the *USA Today* description. "Add lush parks, whale watching and a European-style downtown and this charming city scores high with lovers."

A cynic might argue that "European-style downtown" actually translates to "panhandlers speak French," or "guys pee on the sidewalks." This same cynic might point out that half the people who move to Vancouver Island only do so because it's as far away from your ex as you can get without drowning.

Sour grapes, we reply. We prefer to take the *USA Today* survey as an indication of what a smouldering hunk of passion is the typical Victoria man. (It's true. I asked the women in the office, and they agreed the typical Victoria man is a smouldering hunk of something.)

And how can the critics ignore our romantic ambience: the sun setting on the water over the Clover Point sewage outfall, the enforced tranquility of the two-sailing wait at the ferry terminal, or the candlelight dinners every time a howling December sou'easter drops a cedar on the power lines.

Don't forget our legendary foodie scene, either: nothing says romance like a restaurant with a 4 p.m. Late Night Special. (That didn't escape host John Catucci when the Food Network's *You Gotta Eat Here!* taped in Victoria: "You guys are obsessed with brunch," he told my colleague Michael Reid. "I guess it's because everything at night closes at nine o'clock, so you have to take full advantage.")

This is the thing with rankings. We like the ones that give us the results we want to hear, that reflect the image we want to see. And, hoo boy, does Victoria like hearing how awesome it is. This is a Narcissus of a city, one that could spend forever gazing lovingly at its reflection in the Strait of (Don) Juan de Fuca.

When Amazon.ca, or *USA Today*, or even PinkCherry.com tells us how awesome we are, we ignore the methodology (which might not have been subjected to the same level of peer-reviewed scrutiny as, say, a study in the *New England Journal of Medicine*) and smile contentedly at the affirmation of what we knew all along: we're the best. Even in a country that always hovers atop the United Nations' annual quality-of-life index, Victoria stands out—the city so beautiful that they named an entire long weekend after it.

So we weren't really surprised when Next Generation Consulting of Wisconsin ranked Victoria as the best city in Canada for young professionals, based on earning potential, lifestyle cost, and the social scene. Although we weren't aware that Victoria actually had (a) any young professionals, or (b) a social scene (unless you count the Our Place homeless centre or the boys who jig for herring off the Craigflower Bridge), we had to admit that the Next Gen numbers didn't lie.

Likewise, when the Canadian Council on Learning named Victoria the Smartest City in Canada—based on such factors as education levels, exposure to culture, and proximity to libraries and museums—we just took the compliment as our due. It was an acknowledgement that we're not just pretty, but beguiling in a sexy librarian shaking out her hair kind of way.

(How smart are Victorians? Certainly smarter than the residents of the second-ranked city on the learning index, Saskatoon. If they're so bright, why do they live in a place where the most popular activity is "thawing"? Not that I have actually been there since I was a boy, when the fold-down bed in the Idylwyld Motel folded up and swallowed my sisters, the high point of my life. But I digress.)

We weren't overly outraged when *Condé Nast Traveler* magazine ranked Victoria as only the third-best city in the Americas, trailing Buenos Aires and, for some reason, the pestilential cesspool known as Vancouver.

But we got downright huffy when the Boring Awards shortlisted us for most boring city in Canada. While being considered most boring in one of the dullest countries on earth is quite the feat (kind of like being called the trashiest Kardashian), it wasn't a label we welcomed.

Likewise, we just about went off our nuts when the magazine *MoneySense* ranked Victoria thirty-fifth out of 190 cities in its annual Canada's Best Places to Live list.

Number thirty-five out of 190 might be okay if you're in one of those places that only hits the news when there's a drive-by shooting or the grain elevator burns down, but it's a reason to reach for the Xanax in a city that habitually flirts with the top of any best-of list. Imagine Paul McCartney reading about the Beatles being sandwiched between Def Leppard and the Bee Gees.

Worse, *MoneySense* not only ranked us thirty-fifth, but it placed us behind the likes of Regina; Red Deer, Alberta; and Swift Current, Saskatchewan. We couldn't believe the City of Gardens (our motto: "Just looked in the mirror, fell in love all over again") trailed even Yorkton, Saskatchewan (motto: "Come for the frostbite, stay for the swarming insects"). Obviously, this study was flawed. What were the rankings based on, flatness?

Sometimes, it's best not to dig too deep into the methodology. We were thrilled in 2012 when the *Canadian Journal of*

Economics found Victoria enjoys the best quality of life in the country. Thrilled, that is, until we learned about the measuring stick used to quantify the findings: how much people are willing to give up to live here.

A mathematical formula involving house prices and wages showed Victorians will make sacrifices equal to 17 percent of their income to live in the City of Gardens—a sunshine tax (rain tax?) that reduces us to eating the carpet underlay in homes priced 46 percent above the national average.

Victoria edged out Vancouver partly because, even though both of us have housing prices high enough to make the sultan of Brunei choke on his caviar, Vancouverites tend to earn more money than we do.

That means we have less money to spend on material goods. It's a trade-off. When you buy a house in Victoria, you're choosing to pay for the weather, the view, and the lack of mosquitoes and Toronto Maple Leafs.

"What you're really buying more of is these cultural and natural amenities," the study's author said. "In a sense, it represents a more sustainable way of living."

Yep, that's what we think of when driving our 1985 Chevettes to the grocery store, hoping to cash in on the two-for-one special on gruel: This sure is sustainable. Ha ha, those poor people in Sudbury with their new shoes and colour televisions, sucks to be them.

Which brings us to yet another study, this one ranking Victoria last out of eighteen cities rated according to how content their residents were. Must have been that lingering taste of carpet underlay. Or maybe a data-entry error. How could anyone be unhappy in Canada's Most Romantic City?

Could it be, in fact, that Amazon's conclusion is off and Victoria is, in fact, the exact opposite of the Paris of the Pacific?

Rather than being an indication that our community is a hotbed of heartthrobbery, all those Amazon.ca sales of Michael Bublé recordings and *Hundred-Foot* movies might actually reflect an attempt to make up for a romantic deficiency—an attempt to fill a void.

Given the state of Victoria's men (who might not be quite as godlike as they think), it would only seem logical to seek an online alternative. Being a heterosexual woman in Victoria is like being a carnivore in a vegetarian restaurant; when there's nothing appetizing on the menu, might as well order in some takeout ribs.

Or, put another way, twenty years of putting up with a guy who drinks milk from the carton and laughs when he belches just about guarantees Mr. Darcy daydreams.

Most Romantic City? It might not yet be time to replace Victoria's Captain Cook statue with one of Austin Powers.

As you have just read, Victoria is Canada's Most Romantic City.

Therefore, it stands to reason that its men must be the most romantic in Canada.

How did they get this way? With a little help from Dr. Romance, who takes over my column space each Valentine's Day to dispense relationship advice to the men of Vancouver Island.

Read and learn, boys. Read and learn.

DR. ROMANCE

DEAR DR. ROMANCE: *I just came home to find the house in darkness save for the light of a few candles, in front of which she sprawled seductively. What should I do?*

—*Confused in Colwood*

DEAR CONFUSED: Use your smartphone to check BC Hydro's online map. If the outage hasn't been reported, call 1-888-POWERON.

DEAR DR. ROMANCE: *She came back from the hairdresser and asked, "Notice anything different about me?" So, I said, "Well, you've gotten really whiny since you started gaining weight."*

I thought she would give me points for noticing, but instead she got all huffy like that time I accidentally slept with her best friend.

How can I make amends?

—*Vexed in Victoria*

DEAR VEXED: She might enjoy a romantic dinner. I would suggest starting with shrimp ceviche in phyllo cups, followed by artichokes with roasted red pepper, roast quail with cranberry Madeira sauce, and Campari-poached pears with raspberry sauce. It will take her a couple of hours to cook all this, so you might as well pop out for a beer while waiting.

DEAR DR. ROMANCE: *Is it true that the fastest way to a man's heart is through his stomach?*

—*Mystified in Metchosin*

DEAR MYSTIFIED: Yes, though Mrs. Dr. Romance prefers going straight in with a steak knife.

DEAR DR. ROMANCE: *When she complained that we don't talk anymore, I explained that it's because the things she wants to talk about are boring. She became very, very quiet after that, apparently trying to think of more engaging topics of conversation. Three weeks later, she's still thinking. Can you help us out?*

—*I.M. Toast, Oak Bay*

DEAR I.M.: Certainly. Here are some subjects she might wish to discuss:
a) Can the Canucks go deep in the playoffs without more fourth-line toughness?
b) Your old girlfriends and how much fun they were
c) Who would win a fist fight, Christy Clark or Sarah Palin?
d) Canadian divorce law and the division of property

DEAR DR. ROMANCE: *I tried those topics, but she just started crying. First she wants to talk, then she doesn't. What gives?*

DEAR I.M.: Women. Go figure.

DEAR DR. ROMANCE: *My wife asked, "Dear, do these pants make my butt look big?" So I replied, "Sweetheart, it ain't the pants." This turned out to be the wrong answer. She just stormed out of the house, said she's leaving forever.*

Now I have this piercing pain in my heart, like that feeling I get after eating too much bacon (I know, "too much bacon" is an oxymoron). What does this mean?

—*Dumbfounded in Duncan*

DEAR DUMBFOUNDED: What you're experiencing is called an "emotion." You might have felt the same thing when the Canucks traded Roberto Luongo, or when that supercute cart girl at the golf course quit. Don't worry. Like gas, it will pass.

· ·

DEAR DR. ROMANCE: *So, I should just leave the steak knife embedded in my chest?*

DEAR DUMBFOUNDED: Walk it off, princess.

· ·

DEAR DR. ROMANCE: *I forgot Valentine's. Is it too late to take her out for dinner?*

—*Tardy in Port Hardy*

DEAR TARDY: No. You can even supersize it.

DEAR DR. ROMANCE: *How about a nice glass of wine?*

DEAR TARDY: Thanks. Dr. Romance would like a pinot grigio, please.

· ·

DEAR DR. ROMANCE: *After David Beckham's underwear commercial aired during the Super Bowl, she left fingerprints and drool all over the television screen. Yet when I watched the game in my boxers, she started bleating like that time I used her old wedding veil to filter motor oil. Is this not a double standard?*

—*Slighted in Sidney*

DEAR SLIGHTED: Maybe if you weren't watching the game at Best Buy...

· ·

DEAR DR. ROMANCE: *We were having this great first date at a restaurant, having a totally fascinating conversation about me and how awesome I am, when I noticed she hadn't come back after getting up to go to the washroom forty-five minutes earlier. Since I ate both our meals, can I still ask her to pay for her half?*

—*Loquacious in Langford*

DEAR LOQUACIOUS: Don't ask her to pay. *Tell* her to pay. Women like an assertive man.

DEAR DR. ROMANCE: *She says all she wants is to hear me utter those "three little words." What are those words?*

—Flummoxed in Fernwood

DEAR FLUMMOXED: Multiple choice:
   a) "Pull my finger."
   b) "Honey, you're overreacting."
   c) "Your sister's hot."
   d) "I was wr . . ." "I was wron . . ." Sorry, can't quite get that one out.

DEAR DR. ROMANCE: *Where can a woman find a companion who is loving, is devoted, doesn't stray, and just wants to cuddle at night?*

—Hope Lesley Dreaming, Nanaimo

DEAR HOPE: Try the SPCA.

DEAR DR. ROMANCE: *I am afraid something is wrong with her hearing. What I told her was "Valentine's Day is just a Hallmark holiday, and we should not fall for corporate America's clumsy attempt to extort money from us through emotional blackmail." Unfortunately, what she thought I said was "I never want sex again." When I suggested she go to the doctor to get her ears checked, she refused, saying she just needed a little cry. What kind of remedy is a little cry?*

—Concerned in Cordova Bay

DEAR CONCERNED: Two-teared health care.

DEAR DR. ROMANCE: *You're not a real doctor, are you?*

DEAR CONCERNED: Dr. Romance cures heartbreak and writes prescriptions for love.

DEAR DR. ROMANCE: *Will my feeble attempts at romance today really make up for the obtuseness, insensitivity, selfishness, and other flaws shown during the rest of the year?*

—Saddened in Sooke

DEAR SADDENED: Of course not. Men don't have flaws.

DEAR DR. ROMANCE: *She says most men are as bright as a burned-out light bulb. Is this a valid comparison?*

—Vexed in View Royal

DEAR VEXED: No. You can change a light bulb.

....

DEAR DR. ROMANCE: *I pointed out that the Bible says man was created in God's image. She replied that if God leaves whiskers in the sink, can't turn on the vacuum cleaner, snores on the couch, has a mustard stain on every shirt, and says, "Who stepped on the duck?" when He breaks wind, then she would rather be an atheist.*
    Is man really created in God's image?

—Beloved in Broadmead

DEAR BELOVED: In His dreams.

....

DEAR DR. ROMANCE: *She says she wants me to be more thoughtful. What does* thoughtful *mean?*

—Querulous in Qualicum

DEAR QUERULOUS: You know when you're drinking orange juice and some of it slops out of the carton onto the kitchen floor, so you mop it up with your sock? That's called being thoughtful. It's also thoughtful when you put the toilet seat down.

DEAR DR. ROMANCE: *I thought I was being thoughtful when I lifted the seat in the first place.*

DEAR QUERULOUS: Lift it up, put it down, lift it up, put it down. Women, go figure.

....

DEAR DR. ROMANCE: *I gave her a Valentine's Day card, but when she read the message—"Forever Yours"—she mumbled something about the nightmare never ending, then burst into tears. Should I be worried?*

—Concerned in Comox

DEAR CONCERNED: Don't worry. Women cry when they're happy. Mrs. Dr. Romance wakes up every morning with tears of joy. Great, heaving sobs of joy.

DEAR DR. ROMANCE: *I, too, bought her a card that said, "Forever Yours," so she had me charged with uttering a threat. Should I take this as a hint?*

—*Baffled in Brentwood*

DEAR BAFFLED: No. Men don't take hints.

....

DEAR DR. ROMANCE: *We were out for a Valentine's Day dinner at this superclassy restaurant when I asked her to change seats so that I could watch the Leafs game over her shoulder.*

She did, but got really, really quiet after that, just kept staring at her cutlery. It was a perfect night. Yet when I asked where she wants to be in five years, she said, "On my honeymoon with Justin Trudeau."

What does this mean?

—*Perplexed in Parksville*

DEAR PERPLEXED: She wants you bad.

....

DEAR DR. ROMANCE: *At the end of his first date with his now-wife Sophie Grégoire, Justin Trudeau reportedly finished dinner, turned to her, and said, "I'm thirty-one years old, and I've been waiting for you for thirty-one years." What would Dr. Romance say in similar circumstances?*

—*Sandi in Saanich*

DEAR SANDI: Multiple choice:
   (a) "You going to eat the rest of your chicken?"
   (b) "You don't mind cigar smoke, do ya?"
   (c) "I'm thirty-one and not getting any younger. Pay up and let's go."

....

DEAR DR. ROMANCE: *You didn't get a lot of second dates, did you?*

DEAR SANDI: It's hard to improve on perfection.

DEAR DR. ROMANCE: *I have an algebra question. When Donald Trump married his first wife, Ivana, he was three years older. When he married his second wife, Marla Maples, he was seventeen years older. By the time he hit wedding number three—a star-studded affair at which bride Melania wore a $200,000 dress, Billy Joel sang "Just the Way You Are," and the guests included Shaquille O'Neal, Barbara Walters, P. Diddy, Conrad Black, and, yes, Hillary Clinton—the age gap had grown to twenty-four years.*

Assuming there's a wife number four, how much older than her will he be?

—Math Geek in Metchosin

DEAR MATH GEEK: There will be no age difference. Same-sex weddings are now legal in the US. The Donald plans to marry himself.

DEAR DR. ROMANCE: *The setting seemed right: music, flowers, a bit of wine, candlelight. She's in that classic black dress. But when I cuddle up and start nuzzling her ear, she goes, "No, wait until after church." What gives?*

—Confused in the Cathedral

DEAR CONFUSED: Nuns. Go figure.

DEAR DR. ROMANCE: *My husband forgot Valentine's again, just like my birthday and our wedding date. Why can't men ever remember anniversaries?*

—Pearl Arbour, Esquimalt

DEAR PEARL: They can remember. The anniversary of D-Day is June 6. The anniversary of Paul Henderson's goal is September 28. *Led Zeppelin IV* was released November 8, 1971. The Ford Mustang was unveiled April 17, 1964. There are no other anniversaries of note.

DEAR DR. ROMANCE: *I took her to the dance club like she asked, but when we got there, she stormed out. What was wrong? The music?*

The ambience?

—*Duane Pipe, Port Alberni*

DEAR DUANE: The brass pole.

· ·

DEAR DR. ROMANCE: *I downloaded the kind of movies she asked for—Chuck Norris in* The Delta Force, *Chuck Connors in* Ride to Glory, *Chuck Heston in* Ben-Hur—*but she just got mad and started stomping around like I'd hit on her sister again.*
　　Why is she so irrational?

—*Downcast in Uplands*

DEAR DOWNCAST: Um, that's "chick" flicks.

· ·

DEAR DR. ROMANCE: *Amazon.ca has just declared Victoria to be "Canada's Most Romantic City" yet again. On a scale of one to ten, how lucky are the women of Chicktoria to live here?*

—*Sexy in Saanich*

DEAR SEXY: Eleven.

And just as one more example of how totally
awesome the men of Vancouver Island are...

STREEP THROAT

The men's room at the multiplex was packed. Packed with men who didn't need to go to the men's room.

They shuffled aimlessly, played with the hot-air hand-dryer, made faces in the mirror above the sink—anything to delay returning to the theatre.

No surprise there. The Meryl Streep Film Festival was on, estrogen oozing out from under every cinema door.

These weren't men; they were refugees from movie hell, prisoners on punishment detail. No man goes to a Meryl Streep movie unless he has been caught doing something bad.

"What you in for?" I asked a glum-looking fellow loitering by the cubicles.

"Forgot her birthday," he replied.

"What did she make you go see?"

"*The Bridges of Madison County.*"

Ouch. I winced.

"You think you've got it rough?" chimed in another. "Mine's forcing me to sit through a double-feature: *Sophie's Choice* and *Kramer vs. Kramer.*"

"Good heavens," I said. "What did you do to deserve that?"

"Ogled her yoga instructor," he shrugged.

I nodded in understanding. The classic. I didn't give him any sympathy, though. Like they say, if you can't do the flick, don't eye the chick.

After that the boys started introducing themselves to one another, shaking hands, rhyming off their crimes and punishments.

"Harry Smith. Deleted season one of *Downton Abbey. Music of the Heart*."

"Mike Singh. Broke wind in an elevator. *The Devil Wears Prada*."

"Dave Deschamps. Sat on her cat. *The French Lieutenant's Woman*."

One particularly miserable young guy stood off on his own, hands stuffed in pockets. I decided to draw him in: "How about you, sport? What you watching?"

His gaze remained fixed on the tiled floor. His voice, when he spoke, was little more than a mumble: *"Mamma Mia!"*

The room suddenly went still. We all stared. *Mamma Mia!* One hundred and eight testosterone-sapping minutes of Meryl and ABBA tunes? This guy must be an axe murderer to merit a sentence like that.

"What did you do?"

He lifted his head, revealing bleary eyes, a dripping nose. "I gawda code."

"Pardon?"

"I got a cold. She busted me for being a wimp."

Pandemonium! The men erupted in anger, their faces as flushed as the toilets. One kicked the foosball table. Another threw his beer at the big-screen TV. (All men's rooms have them; don't tell anyone.) A woman can't punish a man for whining while ill! It's what we do!

It's a trade-off. We men accept that we suck at being sick, that our inability to handle even the mildest of maladies opens us to a degree of smirking ridicule. In return for this admission, we expect a certain amount of eye-rolling indulgence, understanding, soup, and orange juice, along with exclusive use of the channel changer for the duration of the affliction. (This is all explained in the excellent BBC documentary *Man Cold*, which you can call up on YouTube.)

Nowhere does it say that an already weakened man should be forced to endure a Meryl Marathon as punishment.

This rankles, even now—particularly now—since at this moment I find myself under the weather: aches, fever, chills, congestion like the Colwood Crawl, weak as American beer, hurtin' like a country song, moaning in harmony with the dog. It's obviously something much more grave than a common cold, though.

"I think I'm dying," I told my wife.

"You sound all raspy, like Burgess Meredith in *Rocky*," she replied. "Say something else."

"I'm serious," I said. "This could be the end."

"Now say, 'You're a bum, Rock,' or 'Women weaken legs.'"

"Remember when I blamed the dog for eating the last of the apple pie at Thanksgiving?" I asked her. "That was me. Also, I might have accidentally slept with a couple of your friends. Thought I should come clean before I check out."

Now I had her attention. "You ate the apple pie?"

"Feel my forehead," I said. "Do you think I'm about to croak?"

"Did you really eat the pie?"

"Yes."

"Then you're about to die."

This reassured me. Frequent readers might note that when it comes to predicting my own demise, my batting average is akin to that of Harold Camping, the California-based radio preacher who on five occasions—in 1988, 1994, and then on three dates in 2011—convinced followers that the end of the world was nigh.

After his fifth spectacular strikeout, Camping tossed his helmet in the dugout and declared himself retired, which must have relieved/bemused/surprised those of his adherents who had quit their jobs in anticipation of the Apocalypse.

Unlike Camping, I remain in the game.

"Stay away from me," I advised my wife, bravely attempting to maintain a stiff upper lip. "I have HV71."

"HV71 is a Swedish hockey team," she said.

"Keep back," I quavered. "I have H5N1, the avian flu. Save yourself now."

I must have been delusional, because her muttered reply sounded like something about having blown that chance more than thirty years ago, so I asked her to repeat herself.

"You don't have the bird flu," she said. "You have a common cold."

"No," I insisted. "A cold isn't nearly dramatic enough. What I have is a deadly strain of poultry-borne influenza. Godspeed, my love. Remember me fondly."

"You don't have bird flu," she continued. "Just like you didn't have SARS in 2003. Just like you didn't have *Cryptococcus neoformans* after driving through Parksville the year before that."

For those of you who are unfamiliar, this is an exotic and serious airborne fungus that showed up on mid–Vancouver Island around the dawn of the new millennium. I was pretty sure I had it.

"You didn't have *Cryptococcus*," she said. "Just like you didn't have Ebola after watching *Outbreak* on the late show."

"What about the time I got anthrax?" I countered.

"You didn't have anthrax," she said. "You had doughnut dust from Tim Hortons."

Yes, well, it could have been anthrax. Just like it could have been H1N1 in 2009, when jittery Victorians lined up for flu shots as though the health authority were selling rides on the last chopper out of 'Nam. On occasion I could also have perished from mad cow, dengue fever, West Nile, and, just to be on the safe side, East Nile.

Today, I am sorry to announce that I am about to be lost to either Middle East respiratory syndrome or the bubonic plague, which appears poised to sweep Madagascar.

For this is the way of the world: we panic out of all proportion to the actual probability of going belly up when the disease is new and sexy, but merely shrug at more likely, albeit more mundane, maladies.

For example, the world really ramped up the hysteria for the H1N1 pandemic in 2009. The Project for Excellence in Journalism found that at one point, swine flu stories took up 43 percent of US network news airtime. Egypt slaughtered three hundred thousand pigs even though you can't get the disease from eating pork.

Afghanistan's only pig, a zoo animal in Kabul, was quarantined. Yet H1N1, while genuinely nasty, was well down the list of leading causes of death.

It seems we only respond to imminent danger, not long-term peril. It's like global warming, where we have a hard time maintaining the appropriate level of alarm about an impending catastrophe whose approach is measured in decades, not minutes.

Same goes for heart disease. It's not the cheeseburger that you eat today that will cause your jammer. It's the one after that, and the one after that, and you can worry about them tomorrow. Anthrax and Middle East respiratory syndrome might not kill you, but deep-fried Mars bars and a lack of exercise eventually will.

Cold comfort to those of us who would prefer to succumb to something sexy, or at least not to something so pedestrian as the common cold.

It's hard for a guy to accept that all he has is a cold, as that means he must also admit that he is a wuss—and must entertain the idea that men are softer than women.

Nothing could be further from the truth, of course. If men are laid low by common maladies more often, it's because we are physically larger than women and therefore have more surface to which the bugs can adhere. If women find that explanation dubious, that's because it's complicated science talk—man stuff like firearms safety and large-engine repair—certainly nothing for you gals to be filling your more delicate heads with. Not like the bubonic plague that fills ours, leaving us utterly helpless when compelled, like the wretched soul in the men's room, to sit through a Merylsical like *Mamma Mia!*

It was with a heavy heart that I returned to my own seat in the darkened cinema.

"You were gone a long time," she whispered. "Missed half of *Out of Africa*. Are you feeling okay?"

"No," I replied. "I think I might be coming down with Streep throat."

Mad as a March hare? On the contrary...

OUR CONTRARIAN CULTURE:

THE NAKED TRUTH

The animal -rights women showered nude, right there on the sidewalk.

Two of them, young and slender, set up a portable stall in downtown Victoria, peeled off, and scrubbed down, smiling as though the odd unseasonably late snowflake weren't alighting on bare skin.

It was a People for the Ethical Treatment of Animals protest against the amount of water it takes to raise livestock, though that point might have been lost on a few rubbernecking young bucks and the one short guy who nosed right in for a close-up, peering over the curtain.

Apparently the women were wearing shorts and strategically placed bandages, but I didn't get close enough to find out. (Journalistic integrity be damned; at some point it's just pervy to look.)

In fact, most passersby passed by without gawking. It takes more than public nudity to get a Victorian's head out of his phone. Parading around as frostbite bait might be a rarity in Ottawa or Edmonton, but naked protesters are to the capital what gun nuts are to Texas.

After all, this is BC, where people have exposed their wobbly bits to draw attention to everything from logging, war, religion, and subsidies for small bookstores, to, of course, antinudity laws.

Here in the capital, we've had antipoverty activists doing cartwheels starkers on the legislature lawn. We had a protester lose his pants at a NATO conference. We've got an annual Naked Bike Ride with more white buns than a bakery. There's a group called the Human Body Project whose members strip down with the predictability of a city bus.

This is why there is no Hooters restaurant in Victoria. We already have plenty of formal dining.

No, to a Victorian a semi-nude sidewalk stunt seems almost, well, Victorian. It's like showing up at Charlie Sheen's house with a four-pack of Palm Bay coolers. Get serious.

For this is British Columbia, the protest capital of Canada. Demonstrating is what we do. Other Canadians grow up gripping hockey sticks; here, it's a No Blood for Oil placard. Family photo albums feature images of Junior's first arrest, right beside the Farrah- and mullet-haired grad pictures. In Ontario, they get up and go to work in the morning; here we chain ourselves to something.

Sometimes, you can't tell the players without a program on the legislature lawn, which over the years has felt more stomping feet than the Grand Ole Opry. Everyone from unemployed mill workers to fish farm opponents to those demanding changes to the province's goat-milking laws (really) take turns. The lawn saw more traffic than Yonge and Bloor during the early years of BC's Liberal government: thirty-five hundred angry teachers one day, followed by a few hundred social workers two days later, followed by two thousand students two weeks after that. ("You can tell who the primary-grade teachers are," observed reporter Barb McLintock. "Their signs are done with glitter paint.")

It becomes part of the province's DNA. Our schoolchildren memorize the dates of famous battles: the Cumberland general strike, the On to Ottawa trek, the Amchitka nuclear test, Vietnam, Solidarity, Clayoquot, APEC, Northern Gateway. BC is the birthplace of Greenpeace (it was a home birth, of course, attended by a Wiccan midwife/aromatherapist).

Credit, or blame, our contrarian roots, wave after wave of settlers—from Russian Doukhobors to American draft dodgers—settling here after butting heads with convention at home.

The closer you get to the coast, the more contentious it gets. More than anywhere else in the country, people in the lower left-hand corner of Canada tend to question authority, reject conformity, and vigorously wriggle out of the warm embrace of Big Brother—particularly if he's driving a bulldozer. "This area has the greatest concentration of tree huggers in the world," environmentalist Ken Wu likes to say.

The Gulf Islands in particular are for people who are unwilling to be told how to think. (A Vietnam-era refugee from New York City once told me how he came to live on Lasqueti Island: "I saw a bumper sticker one day. It read 'America, love it or leave it.' I said, 'Hey, great idea.'")

Statistical proof came from the *Vancouver Sun*, which reported that Gulf Islanders were fifteen times as likely as Vancouverites to reject the power company's smart meters. Vancouver Islanders also skew high in their opposition to the devices. If any of that surprises you, you're not from here.

I don't bring this up to rekindle the smart-meters debate. Heavens, no. As you know, we in the MSM—the lamestream media—have been actively suppressing The Truth as part of our overarching global corporate conspiracy for, gosh, years. (Really, as I was telling Conrad Black while roasting marshmallows/environmentalists at the Bilderberg Group picnic last summer, it's quite tiresome.) So please don't inundate me with proof of how BC Hydro is hell bent on turning my brain into microwave popcorn, or whatever. Thanks, but I eat bacon three times a day, used to smoke, and spent my childhood running through clouds of crop-duster malathion, pretending it was rain. It's too late.

No, I mention the smart-meter story only as reassuring proof of Islanders' continued insistence on stubborn resistance to authority.

Sometimes high-profile protests work, particularly if it is the protesters themselves who are making the sacrifice. The arrest of 850 people during 1993's War in the Woods led to forestry practices changing in Clayoquot Sound. The scientist Dr. Briony Penn couldn't get anyone to pay attention to Salt Spring Island clear-cut logging until she did a Lady Godiva ride through downtown Vancouver in 2001. Victoria's sewage-treatment debate didn't really begin until a mascot named Mr. Floatie began showing up at political events dressed in a big brown turd suit.

But ruin somebody else's fun and your demonstration will backfire. In 2009, activists (including someone who threw marbles in the path of police horses) disrupted the Olympic torch relay through Victoria, ruining the day for disabled kids and others. The Occupy protesters who attached themselves to Victoria's 2011 Santa Claus parade were themselves picketed by a couple carrying a placard reading "Get a life."

Protest camps, which pop up in Victoria every few years (just like Christy Clark) almost always end up being counterproductive. Inevitably, they steal the spotlight from the actual issue—offshore drilling, pipelines, uranium mining, whatever—as the camp gets taken over by tinfoil-hatted crackpots, would-be martyrs, and dogma-spouting ideologues so self-righteous that they make even the most mild-mannered observer feel like clubbing a baby seal to death, just out of spite. The question shifts from "Should we house the homeless?" or "Should we shoot grizzlies?" to "Should the hippie get a job?" (Answer: Yes, yes he should, preferably one in a bongo-free workplace.)

And some causes are more noble than others. Peace, poverty, endangered species, yes. The man at last year's 4/20 marijuana rally in Centennial Square who told me he had to grow dope to put his kids through private school, not so much.

Perhaps, for the benefits of newcomers looking to fit in, it would be helpful to offer a Top Ten list of tips for would-be activists:

1. Don't annoy the people whose minds you hope to change, not unless you're a self-indulgent, arrogant, self-righteous fun-sucker (see Santa Claus parade) who doesn't really care about the outcome. Don't call people pigs. Don't draw Hitler moustaches on pictures of Obama/Trump/Trudeau/Harper.

2. Don't leave a mess.

3. Don't inconvenience others more than you inconvenience yourself. Don't block traffic. Don't block businesses. If you must chain yourself to a truck, at least clean the hubcaps while you're down there.

4. Don't sing. Please. Not "Solidarity Forever," not "Joe Hill," not "For He's a Jolly Good Fascist."

5. Don't chant. No "The people together will never be defeated." No "This is what democracy looks like." No "Hey, hey, ho, ho, [fill in the blank] has got to go." (Though the Portland, Oregon, Occupy movement's "You're sexy, you're cute, take off that riot suit" was kind of clever when the SWAT guys moved in.)

6. Bodily fluids are not toys. Do not spit. Do not pour urine on a city worker while up a tree, as happened at Victoria's Occupy protest in 2011. Do not smear yourself with human excrement while up a tree, as was infamously the case during the Island's Walbran Valley protests of 1991.

7. Come to think of it, just stay out of trees.

8. Don't take your $1,049 iPad Pro to an antipoverty rally.

9. Don't dress up as the endangered species you are trying to save. This is particularly true in hunting season.

10. Keep your clothes on. PETA protesters aside, most people look less like God's image than God's shop-class experiments. Things sag. Things flop, and sweat, and go pear-shaped or concave. Taking your shirt off will not sway decision makers to your side of the fight.

Indeed, shirtlessness is a social barometer, an indicator of how serious you are. You never saw Stephen Harper standing in the House of Commons wearing nothing but cut-offs, or Peter Mansbridge reading the news naked from the waist up.

You do see semi-naked men on TV in hot-dog-eating contests, or making moonshine, or in the back of squad cars. As we know from watching *Trailer Park Boys* and police reality shows, there is a link between shirtlessness and criminality: forget the forensics, just arrest the guy wearing nothing but tattoos. Every episode of *Cops* ends with a tracking dog pulling some squirming, bare-chested weasel out of the bushes.

On the other hand, this is British Columbia, where the normal rule is that the normal rules don't apply. If protesting and acting a little crazy are what it takes to get the result you want, then go ahead. Show 'em you're nuts (but don't show 'em your nuts). Call us nonconformist, call us contrarian, or call us eccentric —we wear it (or don't wear it) proudly.

And that's the naked truth.

THE **HEALTHIEST** (COUGH)
PLACE IN CANADA

Caught a
smoker the other day. He was outside the safe-injection site, trying to make like he was toking up, but since when do joints come with filters?

As you might expect, a mob formed quickly. We pursued him through the streets (we would have brandished flaming torches, but none of us had matches) until he collapsed, winded, about half a block from where he started. Not a lot of drawn-out foot chases with nicotine addicts.

He tried to argue that smoking tobacco is still legal, but that was nonsense, of course. We bundled him onto a boat and banished him to the abandoned leper colony on Bentinck Island. He squealed like a pig when we stapled on the ear tag and implanted the tracking device, but at least we'll know if he tries to come back to town.

This might confuse visitors to Vancouver Island. Is smoking really against the law in Victoria?

Well, no, not technically.

So, may you smoke in public?

No, no you may not.

Unless you want to smoke dope, which you may do with relative impunity. C'mon, every downtown storefront that isn't a hipster coffee shop or vegetarian restaurant is a medical marijuana dispensary—you think they're going to prosecute you for weed?

Okay, I know that last line perpetuates the stereotype of West Coasters as nothing but pot-smoking, yoga-posing vegetarians. That image isn't really accurate, of course. Some of us smoke crack.

But no, we don't smoke tobacco. Or, at least, only one in ten of us do, which is about the lowest rate in the country.

This is a point of pride in Victoria: we're healthy. Or, at least, we're healthy by Canadian standards, which admittedly is like being the tallest midget, or most bashful Kardashian.

Victoria bills itself as the cycling capital of Canada. The city is positively infested with runners, thundering down the trails in soccer-riot-sized herds. Everybody's Facebook page has a mountaintop selfie that says "Look at this view" when what it means is "Look what I hiked up without passing out." We grow Olympic athletes the way Winnipeg breeds mosquitoes.

No one is exempt. Our seniors wear their Fitbits as ostentatiously as Hitler's Brownshirts displayed their arm bands. Even the cop cars have kayak racks. Even the panhandlers squat on yoga mats. Lululemon is considered business attire. Vancouver Islanders do more research when shopping for athletic shoes than they do when buying a car.

Not only do Victorians exercise, but they eat healthily. A few years ago, Victoria was rated the second-most vegetarian-friendly city in Canada, just a bean sprout behind Vancouver. A separate study declared the University of Victoria to be the second-most vegetarian-friendly postsecondary school.

Restaurant after restaurant is devoted to the sale of compost (this description might betray a personal bias). Grocers sell veggie burgers that appear to have been peeled from car tires. People eat kale on purpose, not after losing a bet. If, as reported, only 4 percent of Canadians are vegetarian, then most of that 4 percent are a ferry ride from reality.

They're easy to spot: lean and fit, vegetarians get around on foot or by bicycle, as opposed to carnivores, who prefer to travel by ambulance. (Homer Simpson: "Bacon up that sausage, boy." Bart: "But Daddy, my heart hurts.")

Some Victorians go even further, becoming not just vegetarian, but vegan. Vegans won't eat animal products at all, not eggs, not dairy, not even honey. Their diet consists primarily of small stones and the gum on the back of postage stamps. Vegans sneer at vegetarians the way nuns sneer at other virgins: "Amateurs."

All this is disconcerting to those of us from elsewhere. When I grew up outside of Kamloops—cattle country—there was no such thing as a vegan or a vegetarian. Just as any cyclist over the age of fifteen was deemed to have been busted for drunk driving, anyone on a meatless diet was assumed to be both (a) poor, and (b) a lousy shot. In November, every house had a dressed deer hanging head-down from the garage rafters. It looked like all the other deer had revolted and strung up Moosolini by his heels.

Then I moved to Vancouver Island. Deer all over the golf courses, mowing through gardens like Sherman through Georgia. "Aren't they cute?"

Um, sure.

Wasn't allowed to eat them. It felt like a pub crawl in Tehran.

As one who grew up believing bacon to be a vegetable and preferring food that died violently, I find all this healthy eating distressing. Those of us who salivate at the mere thought of a hearty traditional British breakfast—fried sausage, fried eggs, fried tomatoes, fried potatoes, and fried bread, with salted beef drippings and defibrillator paddles on the side—have become pariahs. Red meat, once the cornerstone upon which every meal was built, has been banned from the Victoria building code.

Certain members of my household, whom I won't identify for fear of waking up (or not) with a steak knife in my chest (though it would be good to see the steak knives used for something), would be quite happy if the fridge were filled with nothing but celery and tofu, the latter being made from the stuff you fish out of the drain when the sink backs up. (I once ate a tofu turkey substitute on a dare from the People for the Ethical Treatment of Animals and ended up in hospital with a burst appendix a mere three weeks later.) Nothing with four legs has anything to fear in our kitchen.

We eat a lot of chicken in our house, but only because it is the domestic equivalent of Switzerland, neutral ground. In homes with opposing palates, chicken is the great domestic compromise, the culinary equivalent of Fleetwood Mac, something not so much enjoyable as mutually acceptable. It's not beef, but not bad, either, particularly when coated and fried in something that clogs the arteries.

Chicken stock (so to speak) went way up after the arrival of the low-carb and gluten-free diets, which knocked all the remaining good stuff off the menu: bread, spuds, pasta.

What's left? Broccoli. Lots and lots of freaking broccoli. Steamed, baked, hidden raw in salad, or stuffed up your nose in the middle of the night.

This is what George Bush (the first one, not the moron) had to say back in 1990: "I do not like broccoli, and I haven't liked it since I was a little kid and my mother made me eat it. And I'm president of the United States and I'm not going to eat any more broccoli."

Broccoli growers responded by shipping him tons of the stuff in protest. (If he were smart, Bush would have followed up with "I also hate single malt Scotch and supermodels.") The broccoli they sent him was given to Washington-area food banks, which is why poor people despise Republicans.

Okay, I exaggerate. There are other vegetables besides broccoli, some of them even enjoyable. Brussels sprouts, for example, are good for hucking at cats.

And corn on the cob not only tastes good, but is fun to eat. To entertain small children, I gnaw speedily down a row of kernels, then make a *ding!* noise like a typewriter. It's side-splittingly hilarious, but the kids just stare at me blank faced. They've never seen a typewriter. Their loss.

But I digress.

It would be fine if Victoria's healthy people were content to indulge their aberrant lifestyle on their own, but they're not. They want the rest of us to live healthily, too.

It's like being in one of those sci-fi movies where aliens inhabit your neighbours' bodies and try to lure you into the fold. "Join us," they chant spookily. "Drink the Kool-Aid." Then they pause. "No, not Kool-Aid. Make it a wheat grass smoothie."

They do this in unison, sounding like those two little girls from *The Shining*. Or maybe the *Children of the (Non-genetically Modified) Corn*.

Runners in particular think they can entice you. They believe that you, too, will become addicted once you hear of its advantages. ("Blackened toenails? Bleeding nipples? Dry heaves? Throw in a prostate exam and you can count me in!") These people include my wife, who has run more than a dozen marathons and thinks it would be a swell idea if I tried it, too.

To which I have always countered with this from the great, late Chicago columnist Mike Royko: "It's unnatural for people to run around the city streets unless they are thieves or victims. It makes people nervous to see someone running. I know that when I see someone running on my street, my instincts tell me to let the dog go after him." (Of course, Royko died young.)

Despite my wife's prodding, the last time I ran with any sense of urgency was in 1981 when chased by a knife-wielding biker in Amsterdam. Today, given the same choice, I might opt for Dutch death.

My reluctance to run might surprise those who have seen my name in the results of Victoria's annual Times Colonist 10K—and with some darn fine finishing times, to boot. I have a good explanation for that: While I might not be a good runner, I'm an excellent enterer, signing up for races, then finding an excuse to jam out and let someone else compete under my name. My best time was set by colleague Louise Dickson's octogenarian father. I'm not making this up.

When I do actually take part in the 10K, it's back in the Big Underwear section, where sweating is considered unseemly and sports drinks are eschewed in favour of a nice refreshing margarita. Some sneer at us, but hey, at least we're out there, which is more than you can say for most citizens of the Great Wide North.

For here's the unfortunate truth: as an obesity epidemic sweeps the country, simply walking ten kilometres is a big deal. The average Canadian couldn't waddle all the way from the computer screen to the ice-cream freezer without having to take a knee en route. (It isn't just us, of course. In England, where they added inches to the width of the standard coffin, health and safety regulations mean some of the more corpulent corpses must now be carried by trolley, not pallbearers. In California, Disneyland had to retool the ironically named It's a Small World ride because the boats kept bottoming out.)

In other words, it isn't that Victorians are really healthy. It's that the rest of the country is in worse shape than the oil patch.

One morning I read a news story so disturbing that I broke into a coughing fit right there at the breakfast table.

"What's wrong?" asked my wife, looking up from her bowl of nasturtiums and radishes. "Got another short rib stuck in your throat? Is your insurance paid up? Would it pay for a trip to Italy? I like Italy."

I shook my head in confusion, spraying droplets of barbecue sauce across the kitchen. "It says here that we are less godlike than dog-like."

It was true. The government released stats showing exactly how healthy Vancouver Islanders are. The grim reality is almost half are overweight or actually obese. Just over half don't eat enough fruit and vegetables. A quarter are inactive. In other words, totally awesome by Canajun standards.

High-five, Victoria (but don't pull a muscle in the process).

Spring has sprung, and there's new growth in the garden, which means—oh no—Buck is back. Vancouver Island has more of a Mild Kingdom than Wild Kingdom, but still . . .

ADVENTURES

WITH BUCK

I unlocked the front door, opened it . . . and froze.

A blue light flickered from the television in the darkened living room. It hadn't been on when I left. Someone was in the house.

"Hands up!" I yelled, brandishing my phone. "I've got a gun."

"Don't make me laugh," replied a voice from the blackness. "If you had a gun, you would have shot me when I ate your lilacs. I'd be in your freezer, not sprawled on your couch."

I put down the phone, shook my head in resignation. Buck the deer was back.

"You always watch TV in the dark?" I asked, turning on the light.

"No opposable thumbs," he said, waving all four hooves. "Couldn't work the switch."

I sighed. "What are you doing here, Buck?"

"Surfing the porn," came the reply. He was watching the Discovery Channel, something about the mating habits of Roosevelt elk. "Ooh, twitch that tail, baby," Buck murmured. Deer are pigs.

I glanced at the fridge: the vegetable crisper hung out the open door, empty as the feeling in my gut. Typical Buck—no fruit left in the fruit bowl, houseplants stripped of leaves, a pile of spilled bridge mix on the carpet. "That's not bridge mix," he said. At least he had the good grace to look sheepish.

Notice he didn't apologize for eating everything in the house, though. Deer have what might charitably be called an elastic respect for personal property.

With a sinking feeling, I looked outside at the garden. Sure enough, every plant was gone. Every single one.

"Didn't you plant any cherry tomatoes this year?" he asked. "Man, I love cherry tomatoes, eat them like candy."

"You eat everything like candy."

Well, there wasn't much he could say to that, not with the evidence just out the back door. Tomatoes, lettuce, sweet peas, geraniums, all grazed to the ground. One minute they were there, and the next they had vanished—poof!—just like the Atkins diet, Napster, and Saddam's weapons of mass destruction. The garden was as barren and lifeless as the surface of Mars, or perhaps Oak Bay after dark. Damned deer.

I know that I am not supposed to be resentful of such intrusions. When I open the curtains in the morning and gaze out at what appears to be the aftermath of Stalin's scorched-earth policy, I am supposed to exclaim, "Wonderful news! The deer have been here!" as though Mother Nature has played Santa Claus and left a bag of treats on the doorstep. A great big, burning bag of treats that get all over your shoes when you try to stamp out the flames.

This is the way we are urged to feel about wildlife in urban areas. Happy. Grateful. Look, it's Disneyland on the lawn, Bambi and Thumper chowing down on another $200 worth of animal food from the nursery. Grab the binoculars for a closer look. Or the rifle scope.

Except Victoria has taken this to a whole different level. Maybe it's the British heritage, all that kind-to-animals, beastly-to-children stuff. Maybe it's all the hippies who subsist on nothing but kelp and grass clippings. Maybe it's all the retirees who treat their pets as surrogates for their faraway children. In any case, the City of Gardens might be the most animal-friendly town on the planet.

Note that a Victoria campaign backed by Vancouver Island's best-known animal-rights activist, Pamela Anderson, just succeeded in driving our last rodeo into the sunset. Also note that Victoria and its neighbour Saanich were among the first communities in Canada—some accounts say they were the first in the world—to ban all animal acts from circuses. Angry protesters routinely mob the courthouse for pet-cruelty cases, but merely shrug at the murder trial next door.

It used to be that our deer were afraid of humans, would only come out in the gloaming, gingerly picking their way through the roadside grass at the edge of town. Now you see them everywhere: your front lawn, Beacon Hill Park, hogging the comfy chairs in the library, "shopping" in the garden centres, as safe as the sacred cows of India.

Having been raised upcountry, in the part of BC where hunters fill their freezers with twenty thousand deer a year, this is still foreign to me. Where I grew up, a deer in the garden was not so much a political problem as a gift from the gods, like a pizza-delivery van breaking down in front of your house.

When I was a boy, we had a backyard swing that hung from a tall frame built out of eight-by-eight timbers. If my dad got a deer, he would hang it from the frame. Once, miffed at the temporary loss of our swing, my older sister plunked me in the chest cavity of a strung-up deer and gave me a ride by pulling on its forelegs. Dad ran onto the back porch. "Hey, you kids, get out of that deer!" True story.

No such impediments to the burgeoning urban deer population in Victoria, where the creatures have no natural predators and hardly anyone keeps a backyard gallows.

You'll spy the deer nimbly leaping schoolyard fences, checking themselves out in the windows along Government Street, texting on their phones, and loitering around the sample tables in the grocery store. (Trust a deer to go straight for the free food.)

Increasingly common are reports of aggressive behaviour to both people (!) and dogs (!!!), raising fears that Victoria's citified deer have finally stumbled across crystal meth.

They're not the only examples of so-called wildlife putting down (or eating) roots in Victoria. Raccoons pry lids off garbage cans. Black bears steal cars. Cougars make their way into town with growing frequency (recently one created a kerfuffle by running laps behind the legislature, which itself is infested with rats, skunks, toads, weasels, and vipers). Barefoot in the park? Not with Canada geese around.

In Victoria, populations of bunnies—an animal not indigenous to Vancouver Island—pop up like dandelions, multiplying like Agent Smith in *The Matrix*. Bunnies are rats. The good news is they are edible rats. The bad news is they are cute. City dwellers don't eat cute.

In 2010, when the number of bunnies on the lawns of the University of Victoria peaked at sixteen hundred, efforts to cull them were greeted with the greatest campus unrest since the Vietnam War. In the end, hundreds were trapped and relocated to a rabbit sanctuary up-Island in Coombs, while hundreds more were shipped all the way to Texas. It took years for UVic to deal with a bunny infestation that Elmer Fudd could have eradicated in an afternoon.

Ditto for our out-of-control geese, the ones wiping out the farmers on the Saanich Peninsula, just north of Victoria. What in the 1970s was a small group of migratory visitors gradually turned into today's resident, crop-destroying population of up to nine thousand birds. They have become a nuisance, fouling parks, contaminating water supplies, panhandling tourists, smoking crack.

The regional government responded with a pilot project in which it managed to break the necks of a total of (wait for it) forty-three geese at a cost of (wait for it) $31,200. As the *Times Colonist*'s Bill Cleverley reported, that was $725 a goose.

"Is it just me, or does seven hundred and twenty-five dollars sound a tad high?" I asked Buck. "I paid eighteen dollars for my Christmas turkey."

Buck raised a hoof, began ticking off the costs. "Well, they had to pay the contractor. Had a veterinarian there, too, plus a 'monitoring consultant,'" he said. "Then there was the palliative care for the geese, the grief counsellors for their flock-mates, the marble for the memorial monument . . . Fortunately, they got a Canada Council grant to cover the interpretive dance troupe they flew in to perform the eulogy."

I paused. "You know you can buy a box of shotgun shells for thirty dollars, right?"

Buck nodded. "And in some countries, you can have a man murdered for fifty dollars. But this is Victoria."

Right, Victoria, where the same people who would happily hose the homeless into the Inner Harbour would just as happily take a bullet for a bunny.

And really, by our standards the goose cull was a bargain. Remember that after the municipality of Oak Bay finally emerged from its deer-cull debate—the longest running soap opera this side of Coronation Street—the result was a total of (wait for it) eleven urban ungulates being captured and killed. It was one of two culls carried out through a deer-management program that cost (wait for it) $270,000 over three years. This is what happens when politicians try to be all things to all people: not much. It's like doing nothing, only more expensive.

This is the challenge for politicians. Whacking deer might be acceptable on the Saanich Peninsula, where the animals that mow through crops like teenagers with their heads in the fridge are, at best, regarded as a doe-eyed nuisance (just like Sarah Palin or One Direction). On the other hand, running for office on the Kill Bambi platform won't win any votes in animal-loving Victoria, where the idea pretty much ranks between heroin dealing and nun punching on the sin-o-meter. When people in tonier neighbourhoods like Fairfield or James Bay say they're having deer for dinner, it likely means as guests, showing up at the front door with a nice bottle of wine and a pretty, partially consumed bouquet of flowers.

Maybe that's because when Victorians think of deer, they think of their pets, which they think of as people. That's not an uncommon approach. A 2012 poll revealed that nine in ten American animal owners believed their pets to be members of the family. Half let their pets share their beds, and more than half buy them holiday presents.

A *Psychology Today* piece based on separate research found people are far closer to their pets today than they were in generations past, treating animals more like children than possessions. Most owners (parents?) know their dog's birthday, the article said, and most keep or display Fido photos in the same way they do of their kids.

The upshot is the more we treat animals like people, the harder it is to find the line between the ones we love and the ones we love to eat.

Dog is on the menu in several Asian countries. Farmers in parts of Switzerland eat both dogs and cats. The French, Belgians, and certain South Americans consume horse meat. Canadians raise guinea pigs as pets, but in Peru they come with a side of potatoes. In Victoria, venison can be added to the list of socially suspect meat.

But then when our deer are joined by one of their less huggable forest friends, when our space is invaded by a cougar, or a bear, or a particularly forward raccoon, urbanites freak out, call 9-1-1 and demand that people with guns rush to the scene and "do something" (in the same way we expected Tony Soprano to "do something"). Then we huddle in our houses until they do, after which we emerge to moan about how cruel they are. ("They didn't have to *shoot* it. Couldn't they have reasoned with it, talked it out of the daycare?")

Occasionally, the authorities must contend with critters right in the heart of the city, as two legendary incidents show:

- One morning in 1989, as twenty-four-year-old Denise Mueller combed her hair in front of the mirror of her James Bay basement suite, a cougar burst through the window, followed by baying tracking dogs and a couple of animal-control officers. It was mayhem: broken glass, busted furniture, flashing fangs, snarls of rage, blood everywhere, just like Bingo night at the seniors' centre. Mueller did the logical thing: she jumped in the closet and slammed the door, poking her head out only after the cougar was shot dead in her bedroom.

· After wandering into the parkade under the Empress hotel in 1992, a big tom cougar was tranquilized. Either that, or he fainted after being handed his parking bill.

You know where you don't find wildlife?
In the wild.
This is not a local issue, of course. The WWF—the one with the panda, not the wrestlers—released a version of its Living Planet Index showing an average 30 percent drop in key animal populations around the globe between 1970 and 2008. The number of tigers fell 70 percent in thirty years. Bluefin tuna are in danger of extinction.

The report blamed overconsumption, saying we are devouring renewable resources one and a half times faster than the earth can replenish them. The countries with the worst ecological footprint per person were Qatar, Kuwait, and the United Arab Emirates, but Canada, at number eight, was right up there. Yeah baby, Top Ten.

So, yes, even as Victoria's urban deer population explodes, the numbers in Vancouver Island's forests have plunged from 200,000 in 1987 to maybe 50,000 today, according to government figures. (Guess we weren't supposed to cut down all the trees.)

Other animals are in trouble, too. Our native red squirrels have disappeared, pushed out by the Eastern grey squirrels that spread like a rumour after being freed by a farmer in rural Metchosin.

The Vancouver Island marmot is so threatened that some of the burrowing rodents were hauled off to the Calgary Zoo to reproduce in safety (though once, after one of the Calgary captives escaped, my colleague Les Leyne wrote a brilliant piece in which he envisioned the little fellow holed up in a fleabag motel, drinking rye, smoking, and plotting his return to BC, the lure of home outweighing the low-tax, high-employment Alberta Advantage and the non-stop sex of a captive breeding program).

I pondered all this, and turned to Buck. "You belong in the forest."

He looked hurt. Or maybe alarmed. Really, deer only have two expressions: placid grazing or caught in the headlights.

"No," he said. "In the forest, I'm food. In Victoria, I'm family. The Buck stops here."

FLYING COWS **YES,**
BITING BUGS **NO**

Stopped on
Douglas at Fort the other day, waiting for the light to change, when this bird relieves itself on my car.

Might have been a gull or, judging by the volume, a Holstein. This was not some little windshield splatter, but a real bumper-to-bumper job. Sounded like a water bomber had unloaded on the roof, looked like a painter had booted a bucket of whitewash off a scaffold. The concussion set off the alarms in vehicles parked nearby.

A small crowd gathered, pointed. A couple of Korean tourists took pictures. Eventually a haz-mat team arrived in white jump-suits, but I waved them off. True, our gulls are a special breed that feeds exclusively on radioactive waste from Washington State's Hanford Nuclear Reservation before migrating northwest and opening the bomb bay doors over Government Street. If you don't hose the toxic, corrosive goop off the roof, your sedan will be a convertible by morning.

But still, my air raid was nothing a Victorian couldn't handle. All I needed was a firehose and Geiger counter. No big deal.

For this is the trade-off we Islanders have grown to expect and willingly accept: big birds for bugs.

This is, in fact, the best part of living in Victoria: the rest of the country might spend May through September being eaten alive by flying, biting insects, but here they are as rare as honesty in Ottawa. No dachshund-sized mosquitoes like in Winnipeg, no northern Ontario blackflies, no no-see-ums. No drenching yourself in DEET, willingly swapping five years of your life for a decent night's itch-free sleep. We see a few end-of-summer wasps, aggressive and unpredictable as Kanye with a microphone, but the offshore breezes ensure that's about all.

Victorians sometimes don't appreciate how lucky we are to live without the pests that make life miserable elsewhere. We forget that there are places where summer means being swaddled in netting, shaking your boots out in the morning, and dropping the toilet seat a couple of times to get rid of the passengers.

When I was a kid in Kamloops, we used to run down the street, arms wide, heads back, mouths open, chasing the low-flying planes as they pumped out a fog of insecticide.

"It's raining! It's raining!" we would cry, faces moistened by the mist. I tell this story to my child, Two-Headed Ted, and he thinks I'm joking.

Tourism Victoria should capitalize on our pestlessness, start marketing the capital not for what it is, but what it is not. It is not, say, Australia, which is less a country than a giant minefield in which absolutely everything can kill you, where you daren't venture outdoors without one of those *Crocodile Dundee* hats with fly-shooing corks hanging from the brim. It is not Mexico, with more bugs than the Soviet embassy. It is not the Canadian North, where campers willingly douse themselves in the kind of insect-repelling chemical concoctions that melt watch straps and cause tumours in rats.

It's not just flying insects, either. Vancouver Island is also free of grizzly bears, rutting moose, lynx, bobcats, and poisonous snakes. What do we have that's dangerous? The odd mountain lion, I suppose ("Woman Who Beat Off Cougar Hailed as Hero" read an unfortunate *Times Colonist* headline). And black bears, though there have only been a couple of documented attacks on the Island. We also have politicians, all sorts of the beggars; once they get into your wallet, good luck getting them out.

But no biting bugs.

Instead, we get eagles, herons, ospreys, owls, turkey vultures, ravens, pigeons, and gulls, gulls, gulls, the latter enjoying a diet that apparently consists entirely of bran muffins and Ex-Lax. But that's okay. It's an exchange we'll gladly make, if only for the entertainment value.

That is, there's little joy to be derived from watching a woman being bitten by a mosquito. It sits there on the back of her neck, sucking like a Canadian sitcom, and you just want to reach over and slap it away, which you would do were it not for fear of another restraining order.

But birds! Good golly, is there anything funnier than watching a seagull open the bomb bay doors on a bald guy? In his book *Neither Here nor There*, the excellent travel writer Bill Bryson devoted much of his chapter on Paris to a description of an ill-tempered companion being taken out not once, but twice, by a French flock, the second soaking being the most awe-inspiring: "I don't want to be too graphic, in case you're snacking on anything, but if you can imagine a pot of yogurt upended on his scalp, I think you'll get the picture." Who needs the Louvre when you've got that?

Several years ago, I was at a change-of-command ceremony at the Esquimalt naval base, where row upon row of officers in dashing dress uniforms were trapped in folding chairs, when this seagull appeared on the horizon.

It came out of the sun, but there was no need for surprise, not the way the officers were jammed in there, unable to move. The seagull seemed to sense this and flew in at a shallow angle, low and slow, wings beating a halting death-march cadence as it lined up the target. A frisson of fear rippled through the crowd, the officers willing themselves small. You could almost hear the silent prayer: "Oh God, not me, not now."

Alas, the carnage was awful to behold, a score or more of Canada's finest young leaders soiled in their prime—a guano Guernica, as it were. I had never seen a seagull grin before. The other ranks agreed it was one of the best change-of-command ceremonies they had ever seen.

The population of urban gulls seems to have increased recently, an echo of our experience with urban deer—the difference being that you need not call Homeland Security's Biological Warfare Response Unit when Bambi gets the squitters.

The temptation, when confronted by these rural-to-urban migrants—gulls, deer, Albertans—is to try to push them away. Scavenger birds in general get this treatment. In the 1990s, Victoria hired a falconer to chase starlings from city hall. (When it was reported that no one knew where the starlings had gone, a grumpy letter-to-the-editor writer replied, "I'll tell you where they've falcon gone. They've gone to falcon Fairfield.")

But Victoria bird expert Ann Nightingale (who has the most awesome ornithologist name ever) pointed out that our winged scavengers serve a purpose. "If they didn't do what they do, we would be up to our eyeballs in garbage."

As opposed to being up to our ankles in bird droppings.

And the tourists think we use umbrellas for the rain.

ROCKED BY

ROCKY BALBEEA

I got shot in the head this week. It was a bee. Flew right through the slot in the front of my bicycle helmet and—bam!—rocked me like *Led Zeppelin IV* as I pedalled down the Galloping Goose Trail.

Couldn't believe he actually flew inside my helmet. Even if you offered that bee a thousand bucks, I bet he couldn't make that shot again. Anyway, I briefly went into a wild Death Wobble, but regained control just in time to rocket into the blackberry bushes. "My, what an interesting development," I said, or words to that effect.

This is what they don't tell you about Bike to Work Week: getting brained by flying insects, big ones, the size of lacrosse balls, the kind that you never expect in Victoria and never see coming until they kamikaze into your noggin at Mach speed.

And this is what you do after a big bug flies inside your helmet: Wait for movement. Maybe it's dead, or maybe it's just stunned, Rocky Balbeea about to pull himself off the canvas, mount a ferocious comeback.

You tilt your head, try to see what's going on up top, but this just makes the bee roll backward, waking him from his daze. Then you feel those little legs churning, the world's tiniest scalp massage, and know what's coming next. So you frantically rip off your helmet while simultaneously trying to beat the bee into unconsciousness before it can sting.

Too late. Balbeea gets me before I can get him. Ow.

This is when the good-looking woman on the bike suddenly wheels around the corner and finds you doing the Bee-Squishing Dance in the middle of the trail, though to her it just looks like a middle-aged man slapping himself in the head in an apparent attempt to silence The Voices that tell him to stalk Jodie Foster.

I tried to explain what had happened, that there was no cause for alarm, that I was merely trying to squish the bee because, well, because I wanted to kill it before it had the chance to die of traumatic stinger loss, or whatever it is that unarmed bees die of, but it was hard to get this message across, what with her blasting me with the pepper spray and all.

Has it come to this? Riding is hard enough for guys like me. In cycling gear, I look as though something went terribly wrong at the sausage factory. Fox News has better balance. Climate change is faster. When climbing a hill, I have to decide whether to have a heart attack right there, or wait until after the dry heaves. Can a middle-aged Canadian man not attempt to murder a bee without being maced by Thelma and Louise?

Well, yes he can, because she didn't really spray me. But she did look at me the way I look at those guys who wrap their heads in tinfoil and talk to fire hydrants. Guess I can't blame her, seeing as the trail has been infested with more flashers than a fishing derby lately.

Anyway, I resumed my ride, but didn't feel good. When was the last time I got stung, I wondered? What if I had an allergic reaction? If I had a reaction, how long would I have to get to the hospital? What if I got there and my tongue was so swollen I couldn't explain what happened and I croaked on the spot, with all the doctors and nurses scratching their heads in frustrated bewilderment?

Worse, what if I went into anaphylactic shock on the way to the hospital, hit the railing on the overpass, and got catapulted into the path of a semi? Then I'd be squished like—ironically—a bee, so they wouldn't be able to do an autopsy and no one would know I'd been stung. They'd just go, "Jack did a header off the overpass. Did he jump or was he pushed?" And my distraught (I hope) family would be left wondering why, why, why?

Well, that last thought made my throat constrict—or was that just the first sign of my fatal allergic reaction?

I was tempted to pack it in right then and there, to curl up in the ditch and wait for the cold hand of death to reach out and still my heart, but somehow my unconquerable will to live kept the legs pumping all the way to the office, where I collapsed at the feet of a colleague, who would prefer to remain nameless.

"Jody Paterson," I said, "I got stung by a bee. I think I'm having a philatelic reaction."

"You're a stamp collector?" she said. "Maybe you're having sticker shock. Ha! Ha! Ha!"

"My tongue's swollen. My throat's constricting. I think I'm dying."

"How long ago did you get stung?"

"Two hours."

"You're not dying. You're thirsty."

Okay, but I could have been dying. I didn't really know what to look for, though, as they didn't have fancy, expensive reactions like anaphylactic shock when I was young. No, money was tight back then, so we could only afford simple bee stings, which were treated by the application of Mrs. Stewart's Bluing, which was kept on the shelf by the wringer washing machine, the one that used to grab and crush my mother's hand. "My goodness, what an interesting development," she would say, or words to that effect. We were poor but happy.

But I digress, as is often the case.

What we're talking about here is killer bees, not the ones swarming up from Mexico and into Hollywood B movies, only to be stopped by the demise of the drive-in theatre, but the lone fanatics that launch suicide missions inside your bike helmet. Must we wait until they're hauling bodies off the bike trails by the truckload before government awakens to this threat?

Like I said, you won't find this in the Bike to Work Week brochure. It's all health-benefit this and environmental-benefit that, not a word about the millions of cyclists slaughtered, or at least potentially annoyed, by flying insects each spring.

Particularly, as I pointed out earlier, in a city without flying insects.

How awesome is Victoria?
They gave the city its own long weekend . . .

GOD SAVE
THE QUEEN

Last we heard, the Queen was bunged away in storage in Saanich.

A Vancouver newspaper called in 2012, asked to have her dragged into the sunlight for a Diamond Jubilee photo, but Ken Lane said no, that would involve dry-cleaning her gown, buffing the royal jewellery, bringing in a hairdresser to revitalize her tresses.

A hairdresser for a wax figure?

Yes, Lane used to bring a hairdresser to Victoria's Royal London Wax Museum every January when the Inner Harbour tourist attraction closed for a few days.

"All of the women got done every year—shampooed, rinsed, and reset," said Lane, the museum's owner.

The exhibits had real human hair, you see. It came from Italy. The glass eyes were imported from a medical supplier in Germany.

Alas, as we reach Victoria Day—a.k.a. the Queen's birthday, a.k.a. the May long weekend—Elizabeth II is nowhere in sight. Victorians haven't been able to set their own eyes on Her Royal Highness since 2010, when the wax museum closed its doors. She ended up in storage with Elvis and all the others who left the building.

Which is, it seems, a metaphor for the way the rest of Canada looks at Victoria: a bit quaint, a bit British, a bit anachronistic, to be dusted off and hauled out of the closet when anything monarchy related pops up.

We are like an aging great aunt who, purple hair askew, lipstick off target, gets plunked at the head table at a family wedding. When William married Kate, the TV cameras descended on the Empress Hotel as if on cue, eager for images of white gloves, pearls, and teacups, maybe some mutton chops and monocles in the Bengal Lounge. Ditto when Kate gave birth, and when the Queen reached sixty years on the throne.

To the rest of Canada, Victoria is the last echo of a long-gone empire; we're the equivalent of a Neil Diamond impersonator, as close as it gets to the real deal without needing a passport or having to drive on the left.

As for our US visitors, half of them expect to see the Queen hanging laundry off the back porch of the legislature, tiara on her head, fuzzy pink slippers on her feet, clothespins tumbling out of the pockets of her threadbare terry-cloth-and-ermine bathrobe.

Only it's not really true, is it? Probably wasn't even true back in 1975, when the provincial government painted the Union Jack on the funnels of the old *Princess Marguerite* and invited Americans to take the ferry from Seattle to what was advertised as a piece of Ol' Blighty. That Britain doesn't even exist in Britain anymore.

While Victoria is, relatively speaking, still a hotbed of royalist support, the monarchy is a bit like lacrosse: it might be more popular here than elsewhere in the dominion (monarchists like the word *dominion*), but it's still not universally embraced.

In truth, many Victorians, just like other Canadians, treat the monarchy as little more than an outdated curiosity. Worse, a foreign curiosity. "The Queen of England," the unwitting newscasters call her, as though Elizabeth II were not also our head of state and a Canadian citizen (which is why you saw her sipping a double-double at Timmy's yesterday).

This is the sort of ignorance that causes indignant monarchists to slop their single malt all over the breakfast table. For the record, her official title is Elizabeth the Second, by the Grace of God, of the United Kingdom, Canada, and Her Other Realms and Territories Queen, Defender of the Faith, Wearer of Plastic Rain Hats, and Mother of Big Ears. Or something like that.

Alas, the only people who still seem passionate about the institution are those who oppose it: republicans. Wretched, grim-lipped, dour, pedantic fun-suckers (I don't mean that in a negative way; it's not their fault that they're totally dead inside), these are the same puritanical zealots who want to ban street hockey, *Teletubbies*, *Harry Potter*, and any mention of Christmas outside the privacy of your home. Their hobbies include worshipping Stalin and burning works of art.

We hear from them each Victoria Day when groups with names like the Citizens for a Canadian Republic or the Humourless Bastards Who Should Devote This Kind of Energy to Real Problems demand that Elizabeth 2.0 be punted.

They even tried to dump the Citizenship Act requirement for new Canadians to swear allegiance to the Queen. "It's a major embarrassment that Canada hasn't yet dealt with this relic of colonialism," the national director of one of the groups said from Toronto (where else but the no-fun capital of Canada?).

No, Victorians reply, it's a major embarrassment that Canada has thousands of old people living in poverty, that we are the highest per capita consumers of energy on the planet, and that we still can't make a decent sitcom. The Citizenship Act, by comparison, is a minor curiosity.

We say keep the Queen, dump Toronto.

Republicans argue that Canada is no longer a British colony, as if we didn't know this, and that our monarchy is illogical. Well, of course it's illogical. All monarchies are until you consider the alternative, which is to replace our constitutional monarchy with some sort of bland, cookie-cutter McCountry where the head of state, head of government, and commander-in-chief are all wrapped into one. There is something to be said for having an apolitical figurehead, one who doesn't, say, invade Iraq by mistake. (Need I remind our American friends that they elected George W. Bush not once, but twice? The first time was bad luck, the second sheer sloppiness.)

Soulless, ideologically driven antimonarchists are slaves to the logic chips that replaced their raisin-like hearts. (Monarchists write poetry. Republicans write instruction manuals.) Republicans fail to understand that the value of the monarchy is not in the individuals, but in the ideals they represent (honour, loyalty, courage, inbreeding, corgi maintenance). As they say in the army, you salute the uniform, not the person inside it. (Except when Prince Harry wears a Nazi uniform to a costume party. Don't salute that one.)

Nonetheless, Canada's republicans have largely had their way for the past half century, quietly sweeping the symbols of the monarchy out the door. The Queen was unceremoniously yanked from every banknote except the twenty-dollar bill (which still comes in handy when she is asked for photo ID). Only older post offices still display her picture.

Not that long ago, the end of every hockey rink in the land was dominated by a big portrait of Queen Elizabeth, her serene face bearing the scars from a thousand deflected slapshots. (In the old Kelowna arena, the Queen's smile was as gap-toothed as Alex Ovechkin's.)

Her picture hung in every school, too, and we belted out "God Save the Queen" every morning. (Some of us still do, though it tends to frighten the other bus passengers.)

What's next? Will we redraw the map to expunge it of place names reflecting our royal past? Haida Gwaii has already supplanted the Queen Charlotte Islands. (Who was Charlotte, anyway?) Regina, we must assume, will also change its name. Ditto for Prince George, Prince Rupert, Prince Edward Island, and Alberta. Two years after that, Victoria will be rebranded as Leningrad.

We in the lower left-hand corner of Canada, the last bastion of the monarchy, have counterattacked vigorously and even achieved a couple of minor victories. In 2008, a public outcry forced BC Ferries to reverse its five-year-old policy of removing the Queen's portrait from ships when they went for refit. And in 2011, Ottawa restored the word *royal* to Canada's navy and air force for the first time since 1968.

Some saw this latter move as an attempt to right a historic wrong, like the Canucks trading to get Trevor Linden back, but we saw it for what it really was: a bid to placate Vancouver Islanders who were still seething after a series of assaults by Canada's military.

To be precise: In 1942 a twin-engine Hampden bomber based at the Patricia Bay airport "accidentally" dropped five unarmed practice bombs on nearby Cordova Bay; one of them plunged through the roof of a home and into the kitchen sink of a woman who was doing her dishes. The Cordova Bay Blitzkrieg claimed no casualties, though records show the RCAF paid $163.01 to compensate for losses that included a sink strainer, three sauce-pans, and a six-inch double boiler (I'm not making this up).

Likewise, in 1996 HMCS *Regina* was conducting weapons tests at the Esquimalt naval base when it "accidentally" fired an unarmed twenty-kilogram rocket three kilometres across the harbour and straight into the shed behind Pete's Tent and Awning, just down from the View Royal fire hall. (Really, it's like living next to North Korea.)

But despite Victorians' valiant rearguard action, it seems Canada's slide into the moral abyss, with the monarchy reduced to an anachronistic footnote, is ineluctable. It is only a matter of time before Canada's ties to the Crown are lost, undone not by the annoying yammering of wretched republicans, but by wide-spread indifference. I say this even though I am, as you may have surmised, an unabashed monarchist, someone who curtsies to dogs named Prince and goes pink at the ears when licking the back of certain postage stamps.

(I also once chased Charles and Diana's limo through London's Hyde Park while waving a notebook and yelling "Mr. Prince! Mr. Prince!" though this was less about the royal family than it was an attempt to mortify my new wife. True story.)

Heaven knows the decline can't be blamed on inattention by the royal family, whose members tour Canada regularly. Heck, they have spent more time in Victoria than Premier Christy Clark.

This royals' love affair with the BC capital goes back to 1939 and a legendary visit by King George VI and Queen Elizabeth—QE2's parents—which included a picnic at Hatley Park, now Royal Roads University. (Prime Minister William Lyon Mackenzie King's wartime diary reveals they later raised the idea of using the estate as a royal residence.)

Our current queen was a twenty-five-year-old princess when she first visited in October 1951, arriving with her dashing young naval officer husband. "They remained at Government House until the following afternoon, when the Duke drove the future queen to Eaglecrest near Qualicum for a three-day holiday," the *Victoria Times* reported.

Imagine that, Elizabeth and the Duke of Edinburgh, just another young married couple rattling over the Malahat for an up-Island vacation—and four months later her dad dies suddenly and she's leading the greatest empire on earth.

After that, the Queen showed up on the Island more often than red tide. She came in 1971 for stops that included Victoria, Comox, and Tofino, where she did some mushrooms, knighted a black bear, and caught a few tasty waves on Long Beach (well, no, but that would have been awesome). Her 1983 trip read like a Loverboy tour: Victoria, Vancouver, Nanaimo, Vernon, Kamloops. She returned to the capital in 1987 and again in 1994 for the Commonwealth Games (though she appeared disappointed to learn fox hunting was no longer a sport).

Her last visit to BC was in 2002. She stopped in Victoria to unveil a stained-glass window at the legislature and in Vancouver to make a cameo appearance at a Vancouver Canucks game, where she not only dropped the puck but bravely fought San Jose Sharks tough guy Owen Nolan to a draw (no, but that would have been superawesome).

Other royals have nurtured the relationship with Victoria, too. Chuck and Di popped over to the Island from Vancouver when they visited Expo 86. Charles returned to the capital in 2009 (this time with Camilla), while his brother Prince Andrew opened the 150th Victoria Highland Games in 2013.

Prince Edward has been here on a few occasions, too, the last in 2014, not that we really noticed—only about two hundred people greeted him at Government House.

Okay, Prince Edward isn't an A-list royal, not like his mother, or Charles, William, Kate, or Harry. Think of Edward as the equivalent to the road company of *Cats*, the one that plays venues like the Red Deer Centre for the Performing Arts and Animal Husbandry (meat draw every second Thursday) instead of Broadway. An Edward encounter is like seeing Trooper instead of the Rolling Stones.

Still, he's a member of the royal family, which used to be enough to get Canadians to break out the bunting and clear the streets of undesirables. Alas, like space launches and Vancouver gang wars, royal visits have lost a bit of their wow factor.

Contrast Edward's reception to that of his mother in 1951, when thousands waited for her to disembark in the Inner Harbour, thousands more jostled outside city hall, dozens of Brownies threw marigolds and Michaelmas daisies in her path at the entrance to Government House, and sixteen thousand schoolchildren waited along her route following a luncheon at the Empress. Really, it was as if Justin Bieber had come to town.

It's a different age now. To watch the sun setting on the British Empire, just come to Victoria and stand on the beach.

A BRIEF HISTORY
OF VICTORIA

A brief history of Victoria, written for the benefit of newcomers (anyone with less than fifty years of residency) and visitors from far-off lands (Duncan).

The city we now know as Victoria was first populated by the Songhees (or Place of Many Condos) people, who migrated/retired here from Alberta thousands of years ago after the great plague of the Trudeau era.

Ancient middens unearthed on the shore give tantalizing hints of a culture built around the trade of seaweed, shellfish, and eulachon oil, the latter lending its name to the famous Grease Trail, a commercial corridor that ran as far north as Costco. (As generations of Victorians will attest, there is nothing north of Costco.)

It wasn't until the arrival of Capt James T. Cook aboard the starship HMS *Enterprise* in 1778 that this way of life came to an end. (Cook died, too, and was entombed in a bronze sarcophagus that stands on the Upper Causeway today. Some claim he can be seen swinging at the pigeons that alight on his head, though these people may be confusing him with that busker who does the human statue routine.)

Change really took hold in the 1840s with British settlement and the erection of Fort Victoria, named for Victoria Principal, the petite-yet-curvaceous star of the popular prime-time soap opera *Dallas*. (As it turned out, this was just her stage name; the Strait of Wanda Fuca, also named in her honour, is more historically accurate.)

The rough-hewn frontier town flourished, its growth driven first by the fur trade, then the discovery of gold, frankincense, and myrrh (also known as BC Bud). A cosmopolitan community emerged, spanning the multicultural rainbow all the way from English to Scottish.

Advances came quickly: Streetlights were introduced in 1883, followed by free downtown Wi-Fi a year later. The Empress Hotel (formerly a Super 8) opened in 1908. The automobile was invented by Emily Carr. The Strait of Georgia, built as a defensive barrier against North America, was completed in 1917.

A high point came in 1925 when the Victoria Cougars, led by the famed Patrick brothers, Russ and Geoff, beat the Montreal Canadiens for the Stanley Cup, inspiring a state of euphoria that lasted until 1929, when it slowly dawned that a BC team would never, ever win again.

This realization plunged the entire province into a period known as the Great Depression, from which it would not emerge until the outbreak of the Second World War, a conflict rooted in Esquimalt's attempt to break away from Victoria proper. It took the construction of a naval base to enforce an uneasy peace that lasted until the violent Desjardins Secession of 2010.

The city received a boost in 1954 when, just to tick off Christy Clark, it was chosen over New Westminster as the capital of a newly united British Columbia. (This landmark occasion was commemorated in the opening of Centennial Square in 1967.)

The flavour of the place changed over time. The late 1960s saw an influx of American vegetarians, losers of the so-called Pig War, flock here from San Juan Island. Their influence on local cuisine remains strong. Other waves brought immigrants from China, India, and—after holdout North Saanich finally abolished slavery in 1973—the Netherlands.

Still, while our image as a piece of Olde Englande exists mainly in the minds of tourists (who, along with salmon, eulachon grease, quinoa, and Nanaimo bars, compose 80 percent of the typical Victorian's diet), vestiges of a colonial past remain. When the Duchess of Cambridge gave birth to Prince George in 2013, he automatically became ninth in line for the mayoralty of Saanich, bumping Nelly Furtado and Jamie Benn down the list.

Today, Victoria is a vibrant modern metropolis with an economy anchored in tourism, government, the military, a burgeoning high-tech sector, and the bathing of old people. Its population stands at 345,000, minus the twenty who were mistakenly shot during Oak Bay's attempt to rid itself of urban deer. Its highest building, the Bay Centre, is as tall as the Peace Tower in Ottawa. Most of its residents live in the trees of Beacon Hill Park.

(All information in this article has been gleaned from the Internet and is therefore guaranteed to be 102 percent accurate.)

It's June, when our thoughts turn to slowing down
and getting away from it all, right here...

THE **BEAUTY** OF **SLOW**

It's hot.
Too hot for work. Victoria is panting through a heat wave.

Okay, so Victoria's definition of extreme weather—anything under seven degrees, or above twenty-two—might seem a little goofy to other Canadians. ("Why, it was so hot that you could fry an egg on the sidewalk, if you had an electric frying pan with a really long cord.")

Still, thirty degrees is rare for us, a gift from God. Combined with a noon-hour start for the baseball game, it's like a direct order from above to go to Royal Athletic Park. To stay in the office would be sacrilege.

In another part of Canada, this would be considered playing hooky. Whenever the television cameras show up at day games at, say, Vancouver's Nat Bailey Stadium, it looks like a police raid at a brothel, guys in business dress hiding their faces and scurrying for cover.

Not on Vancouver Island. Not only are we less likely to wear the corporate attire—shirt, tie, shoes, pants—common to larger cities, but we see no shame in shunning work in favour of an after-noon of sunshine, cold beer, and ballpark franks. (A few years ago at Seattle's Safeco Field, I asked a vendor what the difference was between his five-dollar hot dogs and the three-dollar hot dogs on the street. "Two bucks," he replied.) We recognize that baseball provides food for the soul, too. It provides a sanctuary, an escape from the complications of life.

"You should enter a ballpark the way you enter a church," the great Bill "Spaceman" Lee once said. Lee, described by the *Boston Globe* as "the thinking man's flake," had a fourteen-year career as a major-league pitcher for the Boston Red Sox and Montreal Expos before writing a couple of bestselling books and finding a spiritual home in the Fisherman's Lodge pub up-Island in the Comox Valley.

Anyway, on this particular afternoon, the game is cruising along nicely in the third inning, the Victoria HarbourCats lead-ing the Wenatchee AppleSox, when I hear a voice in the row right behind me: "You can't help but feel that she's luring him into some form of toxic codependency."

Say what?

"I fear that she's manipulating him, which is empowering her, but in a negative way."

I quickly look around to make sure that I haven't nodded off and been carried to a *Dr. Phil* studio audience in my sleep, but no, no, I'm still at the game—as are the two middle-aged women behind me, not that they would know it.

They are ignoring the action on the field, concentrating instead on the nuances of some domestic crisis.

"He isn't blameless," says one.

"No, his acquiescence makes him an enabler," agrees the other.

I turn and fix them with the Big Eye, but the women are obliv-ious. Others in their group pretend not to notice, but their cheeks flush pink under the heat of my withering glare. They know The Code.

The Code says you're not supposed to talk like this at a game. It is no place to publicly dissect private relat, er, relatio—sorry, but this word always triggers my gag reflex—relationships, other than those between pitcher and catcher.

This is even more true at a baseball game than at other sports venues. The hockey rink, home to a game of Sturm und Drang, already ripples with tension. Football fields are sinkholes of controlled violence. Basketball fans are less interested in watching than being watched. The rain-soaked misery of Britain's soccer terraces is relieved only by the occasional riot, usually precipitated by someone rolling up a newspaper and peeing in the overcoat pocket of the person standing one row down.

A baseball stadium, by contrast, is an oasis. While other sports get the blood boiling, baseball—cerebral, evenly paced—has the opposite effect, slowing even the speediest workaholic until he's as sleepy-eyed and mellow as Diana Krall (a good Nanaimo girl) on a morphine drip.

Time slows. Tension flows away. The game is more cerebral than physical, the pace almost languid. It's one of the few professional sports where the people in the crowd might be in better condition than some of the players on the field.

It is, in other words, the perfect Vancouver Island game.

For if there's one thing we in Victoria cherish above all else, it's the value of slow.

Our love of the unhurried separates us from other Canadians. They may see indolence as the devil's work, while we chase it—albeit in unhurried fashion—as though it were the Holy Grail.

Slow living, slow eating, slow driving, slow music. Victorians are slow to start, slow to finish, slow to change (civic motto: We Liked the Old One Better). Our symphony orchestra takes two hours to play the *Minute Waltz*. Our boats have sails, not motors. Traffic cops in other cities have radar guns; ours have calendars.

Other Canadians are wary of grizzlies, wolves, and rattlesnakes, but here in the City of Gardens we fear the banana slug, the pokiest of predators. (Gardening is, of course, the slowest of leisure-time pursuits. "Everything that slows us down and forces patience, everything that sets us back into the slow circles of nature, is a help," wrote poet May Sarton. "Gardening is an instrument of grace.")

How slow is Victoria? The *Globe and Mail* once wrote of it being a place where the word *hip* is usually followed by *replacement*. Even our sporting legends—triathlete Simon Whitfield, long-distance cyclist Ryder Hesjedal, fifteen-hundred-metre swimmer Ryan Cochrane—chose endurance events, not sprints.

Note that at the same time that BC raised the speed limits on many highways to 120 kilometres per hour last year, Victoria dropped its default limit to 40. This coincided with the nearby town of Sidney's abortive efforts to rein in reckless mobility scooters (really, I'm not making this up) and Oak Bay's purchase of portable roadside speed boards, the kind that admonish drivers to take their feet off the gas.

I didn't realize speeders were a problem in genteel, affluent Oak Bay, always thought the Land beyond the Tweed Curtain considered third gear to be something that existed in theory only, like dark matter or Saddam's weapons of mass destruction or Victoria sewage treatment. But no, apparently there are enough scofflaws who get the '62 Austin Cambridges rattling along fast enough to warrant a good electronic shaming, along with a stern "I see you, Basil" stare-down from the volunteer traffic warden.

Anyway, when the non-stop, breakneck action in Oak Bay gets too much for us, we toodle over the Malahat to Cowichan Bay, the first community in Canada welcomed into Cittaslow, the international slow-city network.

Even our natural disasters have a civilized pace. The Pacific Geoscience Centre once revealed that we were in the midst of a two-week earthquake (no, that's not a typo) that would shift southern Vancouver Island about five millimetres—the width of a Tic Tac—to the west, away from the mainland, which we all agreed was a good thing. It was not so much the Big One as the Long One.

Victoria's reaction to this crisis was predictable: we took time for reflection, held committee meetings, consulted stakeholders, commissioned a study, sent the report for ministerial comment, had a nap. Then the Raging Grannies planted themselves on the legislature lawn and demanded to know how the Christy Clark Liberals can justify obscenely expensive earthquakes for their wealthy friends at a time when one in five children lives in poverty.

Mostly, though, we just nodded our heads in approval, for it truly was the most Victorian of calamities: quieter than downtown after dusk, more tortoise-like than traffic at rush hour—rush being a relative term. (The Trans-Canada Highway north of town gets plugged, oh, six or seven times a day by crashes and stalls. The government's response? Erection of big electronic highway signs that warn of delays ahead. This is like responding to a famine by putting up a big billboard that reads You Are Hungry.)

Why do we embrace slow? Credit the demographics. Victoria is a town of bureaucracy and BC Bud, walking aids and wastrels, of old hippies, older retirees, and rat race refugees whose only goal is to slow down (our thrift shops are stuffed with the cast-off power suits of recent arrivals who have traded them for comfier clothing). Ambitious? Sorry, the career path does not lead through Victoria, is not even on the same map.

People who are in a hurry to get somewhere don't come to Vancouver Island, at least not to stay. It is, literally, the end of the earth, as far from Toronto as you can get. The mainland's Tsawwassen ferry terminal serves as a residency test: If you don't have the patience for a two-sailing wait to the Island, better stay on Bay Street. If you do make it to this side of the moat, the signs along the Pat Bay Highway remind new arrivals to drive in metric, take a chill pill, and turn their clocks back to 1967.

In short, there is no reason to go fast, because there is no place to go. Head north and you freeze, veer west and you drown—ugly prospects, but less frightening than the high-speed highways to hell leading south to the US and east to the wrong side of the Rockies. We are more shaken by that prospect than by our slow-speed earthquake.

But don't confuse slowness with laziness, or a lack of productivity. On the contrary, those who move at a steady pace get more done that those who pinball from one distraction to another. (Once, when I was writing a story on Billy Proctor, the legendarily self-reliant hand logger, fisherman, and wise old man of the central coast, his friend Alexandra Morton said something that stuck: "Billy taught me the value of plodding.")

It takes way longer to get stuff done when you're flitting around like a fruit fly on crack. "Much of what passes as multitasking is nothing of the sort: it is sequential toggling between activities," wrote Carl Honoré, author of *In Praise of Slowness: Changing the Cult of Speed*. A British study found the constant barrage of electronic interruptions in the workplace causes IQ to fall ten points, more than twice the loss associated with smoking dope; note that was more than a decade ago, before the spread of texting, Twitter, and public Wi-Fi turned constant communications into an addiction.

That incessant chatter is our white noise; we are no longer comfortable with a comfortable silence. (My father and his brother used to have conversations that resembled two guys playing chess, only without the chess board. Dad was gone eight years before we noticed.) Hyperstimulation replaces thought.

Maybe those Oak Bay speed boards should flash a different message: take your foot off the gas, stop texting during red lights, turn off your phone, don't eat at your desk, chew your food before you swallow. It's summer in Paradise. Get up from that screen and go to a ball game.

Of course, the ball game is better if you don't have Dear Abby and Rhona Raskin exchanging relationship advice in the row behind you, fouling the air with phrases like "facilitation" and "self-actualization" and "what I hear you saying is." WHAT I HEAR YOU SAYING? What I say is watch the freaking baseball game!

If fans insist on talking during the game, they should at least limit their conversations to subjects in keeping with the soporific feel of the day. Batting averages, yes. Relative beer temperatures, yes. Cars, barbecuing tips, fishing, yes, yes, yes. Relationships, no. Politics, no. Business deals, no. Céline Dion, no, no, no, no, no.

I closed my eyes and prayed really hard, but the batter failed to line a foul ball into the noggin of either woman, which caused me to lose a little bit of my religion.

Deep breath, I told myself. Slow down.

LEAVING **PARADISE**

We were just about ready to not leave on holiday. Time for the last-minute panic.

As usual, I had left the organization up to her, so was pretending not to notice the accusing glances as she quickly ran through the list: toothbrushes still in the bathroom, sleeping bags still under the stairs, blow dryer still packed away (as if I cared).

"Is the iron plugged in?" she asked.

"No, I'll do it now."

"What time didn't we make the ferry reservation for?"

"The ten o'clock sailing."

"Do we have time to make it?"

"Not a chance."

"So we saved seventeen fifty by not losing a reservation we didn't make?"

"Yes."

High-fives all round.

This, dear reader, is the beauty of the staycation: No deadlines. No packing. No ferry fares.

When you spend your holiday in your own home, there are none of the hassles of hitting the road. No insects. No in-laws. No sand in improbable places. No airplane meals prepared in another country/century, then reheated/resurrected like Lazarus lurching up from the dead.

No sleeping on Cousin Eddie's Hide-A-Bed, the one with the metal bar across the middle that feels like Zdeno Chara is cross-checking you in the kidneys all night long. ("Good news! Jumbo's parole came through. Of course that means you'll be double-bunking tonight. No spooning.")

No midnight pleading for a room in the last fleabag motel on the highway, the one that still advertises COLOUR TV, each fading letter on the sign painted a different hue. No leaving friends behind; as Dan Hicks sang, "How can I miss you when you won't go away?"

Some say the term *staycation* was coined by Brent Butt in a 2005 episode of *Corner Gas*, the one in which he vacationed in a lawn chair across the road from his gas station, penning postcards to the folks back home.

But we on Vancouver Island like to claim it as ours. For really, why would we want to holiday anywhere else? Why would we want to leave a place that the rest of the world flocks to as a paradise? Why would we go to the expense and effort of trying to leave one of the most inconveniently placed parts of Canada? (Our motto: You Can't Get There from Here.)

Of course, we all have to learn this lesson the hard way, having first embarked on the traditional Trans-Canada Holiday from Hell, the one that begins with the kids in the back seat, the canoe on the roof, the tent in the trunk, and the tent poles back on the front steps, right beside Dad's wallet and the canoe paddles.

It's pretty much the same rite of (potholed) passage all Canajuns take, but when you start the trip from way out in left field (a.k.a. Victoria), this journey means an extra couple of days of driving, all the way to Much Too Flat, Manitoba, and back without once stopping to pee. The Prairies keep rewinding like *Groundhog Day* out the window: a field of wheat, a field of flax, a field of summer fallow. A field of wheat, a field of flax, a field of summer fallow. A field of wheat . . . The hottest weather you'll see is during the three-sailing wait at the ferry terminal.

And oh, the joy of the modern family bonding: one child watching a movie on an iPad, another texting to her friends about how bored she is, another nodding away behind closed eyes to whatever is playing on his phone. Meanwhile, over in the front passenger seat, Snookums clicks away on a laptop computer, catching up on a few loose ends from work, oblivious to either scenery or companions. After a couple of hours of this, you have to check the rear-view mirror to see if Chevy Chase is staring back. Glad we had this time together, folks. Don't forget to tip your driver as you exit the vehicle.

If a family does want to buck the tide and holiday on the mainland, here are some of the expenses they face:

- Start by packing the car. Cooler: $42. Five-man tent, purchased to cut hotel costs: $289. Sunblock: $9. Assortment of egg salad and tuna sandwiches for first day: $8.

- Tank of gas when you leave Victoria: $50.

- Prairie road map, which Dad leaves at home because "only an idiot could get lost in Alberta": $7.25.

- Take secret shortcut from ferry to Fraser Valley freeway, but become confused. Fine for crossing border illegally: US$275.

- Stop at roadside stand to buy Fresh-Pressed Okanagan Apple Juice: $17.

- Okanagan apples don't ripen until fall. Murky, lukewarm juice was Fresh-Pressed when Kim Campbell was prime minister. Rolaids: $1.50.

- Value of food in cooler: $37.

- Value of food in cooler that will either freeze, get smooshed, rot, or get soaked when the pickle jar leaks: $35.

- Happy Meals bought following cooler crisis: $16. (By the way, when the sign by the highway says the next restaurant is only 30 minutes away, it means by air.)

- Cost of soggy cheese, mayo, and pickle juice sandwich hastily built after coming up one Happy Meal short: 47 cents.

- Medical costs after confusing sunblock with mayo: $54.

- Reservation fee for Whispering Shores campground: $15.

- Loss of reservation fee after discovering Whispering Shores campground is bordered by the Trans-Canada, the railway, an all-night truck stop, and the pulp mill settling ponds: $15.

- Tenting fee at Moonlit Waters campground: $45. There are no waters, but lights from landing passenger jets simulate moonlight.

- Chiropractor's bill after Dad spends night in car: $75. (Helpful hint: A five-man tent really will sleep five people comfortably, as long as they are dead. It will also sweat and weep like Pavarotti in *Pagliacci*.)

- Boat rental, rod, tackle, fishing licence, camcorder dropped overboard at Angry Mosquito Lake: $769.

- Value of rainbow trout caught at Angry Mosquito Lake: $1,931 a pound.

- Fine for retention of undersized trout: $250.

- Shrewdly wait to fill up on cheap Alberta gasoline. Savings: 19 cents a litre. Run out of gas just over provincial border, seventeen kilometres shy of closest service station.

- Stop in Dog Lick, Alberta, for Annual Celebration of Livestock Abuse. Family pass to rodeo: $45.

- Leave rodeo in a hurry after child tells locals she is vegetarian and animal sports are barbaric. Refund: $0. Tar and feathers: Free.

- One night's accommodation in the Wild Rose Roadside Rest Motel and Autobody ("Pool. Clean sheets on Wednesdays. Hot water available until 4 p.m. Free shuttle bus to regional correctional centre. Welcome,

Canadian Association of Bagpipers!"), which Dad discovers while not getting lost in Alberta: $91.

- Turns out "pool" referred to eight-ball table in the pub. Spend $18 in loonies, and leave kids watching $7.50 pay-per-view movie—*Free Willy*—in the room.

- Turns out this version of *Free Willy* has nothing to do with a whale. Child therapist: $85 an hour.

- Scotch whisky: $40. This may not seem like a necessary expense until you consider the following five-way conversation:

  "Are we there yet? I have to pee."
  "I asked you if you had to go at the gas station."
  "Dear, that was in Saskatchewan."
  "When I was a boy, we could hold it for four provinces."
  "Dad, when you were a boy, there were only four provinces."
  "Don't make me come back there!"
  "I still need to pee really bad!"
  "Mum, she's looking out my window again! Make her stop!"
  "Mum, the dog threw up on your sleeping bag!"
  "Mum, why is the oil light on?"
  "Um, I don't need to pee anymore."
  "Mum, why are you crying?"

- Back in BC, gas station sign reveals new price structure: "Regular unleaded, $1.52 per hundred grams. 7 percent financing OAC. Easy monthly payments."

- Arrive at Pristine Waters Wilderness Retreat. Turns out the only pristine waters are in the Shower Shack ($2 for three minutes, $5 if you want it hot), and the wilderness is, indeed, in full retreat. Resort looks like a Costco parking lot without the Costco. Loss of deposit: $75.

- Conciliatory ice cream treats after angrily threatening to have worst-behaved family member expelled from the trip, just like on *Survivor*: $16.

- Bus fare from Revelstoke after family votes you out of the car: $113.
- Arrive home. Find egg salad and tuna sandwiches still on kitchen table. Cleaning supplies, gas masks: $79.

No, much better to stay at home and simply pretend you're somewhere else: Go for a drive and get lost (but don't admit it). Pay for your meal in US currency, then moan about the exchange rate. Better still, call your spouse on the other line and ask for room service. Sleep until noon, then leave instructions on the door: "Please make up this room." Eat brunch, but leave the dishes on the table. Then go for a relaxing run—a really fast one, if you know what's good for you.

She gave me The Look: "You're driving me crazy."

To which I replied: "Are we there yet?"

MY ILLICIT LOVE:

BC FERRIES

We have reached summer—tourist season —and I have a deep, dark secret to reveal: I like BC Ferries.

This is not something you're supposed to admit when you live on Vancouver Island. It's akin to confessing to a fondness for Mel Gibson, Nickelback, or American beer.

Hating on BC Ferries has, in fact, been a British Columbian birthright—just like cross-border shopping or cutting firewood without a permit—since the provincial government launched the service in 1960.

The ferry corporation is a great big monopoly upon which we are utterly reliant and helpless to defy, which makes us resentful. You can't drive on or off The Rock (or the surrounding Little Rocks) without fitting into its schedule or paying what it chooses to charge, which is a lot. The cost of hauling a family of four from civilization (the Island) to Toronto-by-the-Sea (Vancouver) is roughly equal to the debt of a small Third World nation.

Everybody has a reason to be angry. The Liberal Party is outraged when there's political interference in running the ferries, and the New Democratic Party is outraged when there isn't. (The Greens are just mad that the ships aren't rigged with oars and sails.)

Unionized British Columbians are offended by the Bill Gates-like salaries of senior Ferries management, while private-sector types grumble about the Bill Gates–like wages of Ferries cafeteria workers (who point out that they double as first-aid attendants, which comes in handy when the customers choke on the prices).

Me, I bleat like a wounded goat every time I surrender my credit card at the ticket booth (you might also hear some muffled moaning from the passengers hidden in the trunk).

Still, I can't help it: I like BC Ferries.

I like the spiffiness of the ships. I like the metronomic efficiency of the service, and the friendliness of the crew. I like the way the tourists gawk at the postcard-after-postcard scenery sliding by as the ships sail through the Gulf Islands, and the way Albertans break down in tears upon realizing they have to go home.

It's easy to spot the Islanders on the ferry. We all rush to find our preferred seats, then spend the entire passage with our heads jammed in our iGadgets, as though YouTube or Facebook had half as much to offer as the view from the deck.

Tourists, on the other hand, gaze out the windows in slack-jawed wonder. In some ways, having them ride our ferries is like inviting them into our living room. We beam with pride whenever they *ooh* at an eagle or *aah* at that dream house perched above an island shore, as though we were responsible for the splendour.

Sometimes our visitors pose questions we should be able to answer, but can't: "What's that island on our left?"

What we should do is admit our ignorance and go study the wall map again. But no, we don't want to look bad, so we make it up. "On our left? Oh, you mean port. That's Galiano, named after a Spanish sea captain who steered his ship onto its shores after drinking too many Harvey Wallbangers."

We also pretend not to be excited when orcas appear off the bow. Instead, we strike a Suzuki-like pose of West Coast eco-chic sophistication, nod sagely, and murmur, "Ah, J pod's back."

Natural beauty aside, there are the well-appointed vessels themselves, which are positively palatial in comparison to the utilitarian hulks down in Washington State. (Or how about those English Channel ferries, where passengers rush to the bar and pound back as much liquor as they can, as fast as they can, in preparation for the rigours of driving on the wrong side of the road in a foreign country.)

Admit it, Islanders, our newer ferries are pretty nice—though you feel a tad chagrined when you lose the roll of the dice and find yourself aboard the *Queen of Asbestos* instead. That's the ferry they only dust off and pull into service when they really have to, the one with the insulation hanging from the ceiling and the interior design by the same guy who did the Soviet prison system. I always felt apologetic when tourists would climb its too-narrow stairwell and emerge into what appeared to be a 1960s bus depot waiting room.

I once found myself on the *Asbestos*, standing in the concession line with a European woman who was staring in consternation at some packaged food that looked older than she did.

"You should see the other boats," I wheedled. "They're really nice. Got flush toilets and everything."

European woman smiled politely, clutched her purse, and scuttled away. She didn't believe me. I hung my head in despair, feeling we had failed the guest test. My muffin, also ashamed, wept gently in its cellophane wrapper.

I think all of the *Asbestos*-class boats have actually been scuttled now, as have the more frightening food items sold on the ferries. Today's menu ranges from healthy fare to the good stuff where you lick the grease off your arms for dessert.

Long gone is the legendary/notorious Sunshine Breakfast, a universally scorned but inexplicably popular concoction featuring a toxic Day-Glo yellow sludge (Hollandaise sauce, Chernobyl-style) slopped on twin balls of reconstituted egg-like substance. (Can't you just taste it still? If so, put your head between your knees and the sensation will soon pass.)

Victorians driving south on the Pat Bay Highway used to think it a public service to hang out their car windows and holler, "Don't eat the Sunshine Breakfast! Don't eat the Sunshine Breakfast!" at ferry-bound tour buses.

I even wrote a song about the dish once, sung to the tune of "The Wreck of the Edmund Fitzgerald":

You'd best look aghast at the Sunshine Breakfast
'Cause the washrooms are all closed for cleaning.
The yellowish dregs that they pour on your eggs
Will give Active Pass a new meaning.

I felt kind of bad in 2003 when the ridicule finally killed off the Sunshine Breakfast, which I now miss in the same way I miss Tiger Williams, my old ugly dog of a pickup truck, and anything else that's simultaneously familiar, endearing, and slightly embarrassing in polite company.

But I digress.

The best thing about BC Ferries is its system of justice.

In a world where it takes five years to bring Stanley Cup hockey rioters to trial, where political contributions buy government concessions, where criminals receive not just a second chance but a thirty-fifth, thirty-sixth, and thirty-seventh, it is comforting to know that someone is getting it right.

To be specific: High above the parking lot at the ferry terminal, an eagle-eyed BC Ferries employee gazes down from the control tower, ready to mete out swift, sure, and impartial retribution on any driver with the temerity to budge in line.

Some places accept butting in (or budging, if you prefer) as a way of life, with people shoving and jostling like sausage sample day at the supermarket. These are generally the same countries where a succession of colonels take turns being president-for-life.

Not here, not in an ultra-orderly government-and-military town like Victoria, where we recognize that when the rule of law fails, society begins to crack. Respect for authority crumbles. One minute you have unchecked line-budging, next thing you know it's a dystopian nightmare, roving gangs of feral youth knocking over liquor stores and preying on the weak and aged. Things fall apart; the centre cannot hold.

We need to believe that cheaters seldom win, that the bad guy will be convicted in the last ten minutes of *Law and Order*. Do the right thing—pay your taxes, pick up after your dog, return lost wallets, wait your turn—and you will go to heaven. Budge in line and you will burn for eternal damnation.

Alas, the justice system fails us all too often (I once saw a guy with fourteen items in his grocery cart try to brazen his way through the Nine Items or Less line, but when I called 9-1-1, the police refused to fulfill their duty). Happily, though, BC Ferries is there to restore our faith.

For if someone sneaks into the wrong lane at the ferry terminal—bam!—the Tower Gods jump the offender like a cougar taking out a house cat. The loudspeaker booms, "You in the grey Jaguar in lane five, get to the back of lane thirty-eight." And then the guy at the wheel of the Jaguar does the Drive of Shame—his wife and children cringing from the public humiliation—all the way to the back of the line, where orange-vested workers paint a big scarlet letter on the hood (okay, I made up that last bit, but it's a nice thought). Sometimes when you witness this, you can actually hear people in other cars cheering.

Lord, but this is satisfying. It's the kind of retribution we haven't seen since BC's most famous jurist, Judge Matthew Begbie, tamed the wild frontier in the nineteenth century. (History buffs will recall that during the Cariboo gold rush, Begbie once sentenced an American murderer to death. When the murderer announced that he would appeal, Begbie replied: "It will take six months or more for the colonial secretary to deal with the matter and months more before we learn of his decision. But you will not be interested in what he decides, for you are to be hanged Monday morning." Excuse me, but that story always makes me a little misty.)

But again I digress.

As much as there is much to love about riding the ferries, there are still things that drive us nuts—such as the other passengers.

Inevitably, on a crowded sailing, you get stuck beside one of those people who bellow into their phones as though no one else is around.

Not long ago, after boarding the boat in Tssawwaswwasesen (or however it's spelled), I found myself sitting beside a young fellow who, according to his voluble conversation with an unseen friend, was going to Vancouver Island "to get wasted."

It seems he was disgruntled. The girl of his dreams, or at least of the previous night, had failed to provide him with the full range of services to which he felt entitled. He described, in graphic detail, what she did and did not do, his assessment delivered in the plaintive tones of a man whose new car had been delivered without the promised undercoating—though, frankly, after listening to him rhyme off a package of extras that included the sexual equivalent of on-board entertainment, seat warmers, and a backup camera, it was hard not to feel he was nitpicking.

All this he conveyed—going into such detail that it was hard to follow without a copy of *Gray's Anatomy* and a laser pointer—with no regard to the hundreds of passengers squirming within earshot. It wasn't until the end of the call that Randy, as I dubbed him, showed a desire for discretion. "Keep it on the down low!" he hollered into the phone, loudly enough to rattle the windows. Outside, seagulls covered their ears with their wings. Earthquake scientists scrambled for their seismographs.

Occasionally, your fellow passengers will be even more disruptive. In 2005, a man holding two inflated garbage bags jumped off the *Spirit of British Columbia* in Active Pass and swam for shore. It turned out he was late for a big baseball game, so rather than get off the Tsawwassen ferry at Swartz Bay and board another vessel home to Mayne Island, he took a shortcut. He was lucky to survive. No word on who won the game.

Much more common, but always annoying, is the car-deck chaos that happens at the end of every sailing on the mainland–Vancouver Island routes.

It follows the same routine every time: At the first sighting of the terminal, a lookout in the crow's nest yells, "Land ho!" and drivers stampede to their vehicles. Someone taps her brakes, the tail lights flash red, and the impatient man behind her fires up his engine like he's the white-knuckled getaway driver and Bonnie and Clyde are racing out of the First State Bank of Okabena with guns blazing. Immediately, every other driver on the ferry follows suit, transforming the car deck into the roaring, thundering starting grid at Talladega Superspeedway, v in an echo chamber. Never mind that the ferry has yet to reach shore. "Gosh," says the captain. "They seem to be in a hurry. I guess I should go faster."

But, wouldn't you know it, BC Ferries frowns on its boats hitting the beach at thirty knots, so the docking process inches along at granddad-with-a-walker speed. Nonetheless, the passengers keep their cars idling, spewing exhaust like a coal-fired power plant, because, you know, running the engine for eight minutes while going nowhere is somehow going to shorten the snail's-pace race down the highway after they disembark. (It's around this point that Elizabeth May loses her will to live.) Good thing all this gunning of motors isn't taking place in an enclosed space or anything, otherwise it might fog our brains and affect our decision-making ability.

Periodically, all this will lead someone to suggest replacing the ferry system with a fixed link between Vancouver Island and the less fortunate part of Canada. Look at Confederation Bridge, they say, the one connecting Prince Edward Island to, um, Labrador? (West Coasters are a bit iffy on their Eastern geography.) We should have a bridge, too, they argue.

That will rouse the other side: Why would we want a bridge when we just made our last payment on the moat? Besides, coming to an island and then demanding a bridge is like buying near a farm and complaining about the smell of manure.

This topic is the ultimate antidote to a slow news day on Vancouver Island: nothing fills the letters-to-the-editor page like the question of whether to span the strait. Every couple of years, someone suggests building a bridge linking paradise to the over-populated, frantic, pucker-butted, pestilential cesspool on the other side of the water (not that I mean that in a negative way), and next thing you know, they're hooting and hollering in the hottest debate since that white-and-gold or blue-and-black dress was on the Internet.

For now, at least, we have BC Ferries, and I am glad. Bon voyage.

O, Canada, you look a little different from over here . . .

CHERS TOURISTES

Dear American visitors/*Chers touristes américains*, On behalf of the Government/*Gouvernement* of Canada, I would like to say welcome/*bienvenue* to Vancouver Island/*L'Île de Fantasy* and the Great White North/*Grand Pink Bit sur le Map*.

As you might have noticed while surrendering your firearms to the Canada Border Services Agency/*Bureau du Cherche de la Cavité*, ours is a country that enjoys its own laws and customs, some of which may differ from yours.

The first thing you will notice is how much nicer we are than you. And politer. And more modest. Waaay more modest. Just ask us. Actually, you don't have to ask, we'll chase you into your hotel lobby to boast about how famously self-effacing we Canadians are. Sorry.

That's something else you'll notice: like Justin Bieber, we like to say *sorry*. A lot. In their book *How to Be a Canadian*, Ian and Will Ferguson devoted an entire chapter to what we really mean when we do so. (For example, "Sorry, I didn't see you" translates to "I'm in a hurry and you're in my way.") The Fergusons offer twelve such examples, concluding, "Canadians say 'sorry' an awful lot, but they rarely apologize."

Given our humility, for which we apologize, you might think it strange that we are given to ostentatious demonstrations of flag-waving pride (to clarify, that's non-rainbow pride, though we're also rainbow proud, if only to show how morally superior we are, or at least were until you finally caught up with us and legalized same-sex marriage, ruining our fun).

Upon your arrival today, you might have been taken aback by the number of maple leaves you saw flying from cars, decorating storefronts, covering grow-op windows, and tattooed on the cheeks (facial and otherwise) of ordinary Canadians.

That's because you have landed here on the eve of our national celebration, Canada Day/*Fête du Face Painting*, when citizens from coast to coast to coast are united by a single goal: stretching a mid-week statutory holiday into a superlong weekend.

In the midst of this festival of heritage, you might pause to ask just what it is that Canadians are so proud about. Here are some of the things we think are worth celebrating:

- We rank sixth in the entire world on the global Prosperity Index, based on such measures as health, personal freedom, education, safety, and security.

- Our average life expectancy is almost eighty-two years, near the top.

- We live free of the endemic corruption that cripples other countries.

- The World Health Organization says we have the third-cleanest air on the planet.

- Statistically, we have the most living space of anyone on earth, an average of 2.6 rooms per person.

- We invented sonar, insulin, Easy-Off oven cleaner, and the egg carton.

- Our prime minister, while a little shaky with the budget-balancing math, is hotter than a twenty-dollar Craigslist iPad.

Canada is the world's second-largest country by area, after Russia, or maybe Walmart, ranging from the US border in the south to the top of the atlas in the north.

Our dominion has the world's tenth-largest economy, behind the US and China, but just ahead of J.K. Rowling. It has a population of 35 million people, most of whom you will find in front of you at the BC Ferries terminal. For this, we apologize. (There's that endearing contrition again!)

Although we look and speak like you, culturally we enjoy many differences. Indeed, many Americans find Canada a bit of a puzzle. To quote Winston Churchill: Canada is a riddle wrapped in a mystery inside an enigma, dredged in flour, coated in bread crumbs, and baked at 350 degrees Fahrenheit for an hour. (Sir Winston was feeling peckish at the time.)

With that in mind, you will want to pay heed to this, an American's Guide to Canada.

CURRENCY

You might be pleasantly surprised to find your dollar stretches much further here, thanks to the relative weakness of the Canadian dollar, also known as the loonie, which is why one side of the coin features an image of Donald Trump in profile (just kidding; put it back in the holster, Tex). Nonetheless, you might also be surprised to find it costs as much to fill up on gas in Canada as it did to buy your whole car back in the US.

You may also notice that our currency also differs from yours in size, colour, and denomination. Much of it is printed by the Canadian Tire Corp. and bears the image of our monarch, whom you will of course recognize as our beloved King Hamish III. This is special money, and should be exchanged at par with the US dollar. Really. Trust us.

Canada's contribution to the world's cuisine: maple syrup, rye whisky, pemmican, instant mashed potatoes, and ketchup chips.

Sorry (see "Fergusons," above).

Actually, we do have good dishes, but they tend to be regional. Newfoundland has screech and seal flipper pie. Maritimers' diets are made up almost wholly of lobster, except in Prince Edward Island, where the land mass is 50 percent potato. Quebec has tourtière, Montreal smoked meat, and the fries-gravy-and-cheese-curd concoction known as poutine (literal translation: heart attack in a bowl). In Ontario, they eat beaver tails while skating on the Rideau. Yes, real beaver tails. We think. Prairie people subsist on nothing but wheat, saskatoon berries, and hockey rink hot dogs. Up north, they ward off scurvy with birch bark tea and sourtoe cocktails.

Here on Vancouver Island, we're famous for sockeye salmon (which gets its name from the Salish *sukkegh*, or "red fish"), the combo burger (your basic US-of-Eh hamburger, with a sliced wiener added), and our greatest contribution to global cuisine, the Nanaimo bar.

We tend to take this homegrown treat for granted, most of us not even aware of its ingredients. ("I'll tell you what's in a Nanaimo bar," sang Gabriola Island folk singer Bob Bossin. "Smoke and peelers, cocaine dealers, redneck loggers, non-stop talkers, hookers with daughters, yes, yes, yes.")

Truth is, the Nanaimo bar, sweeter than Sidney Crosby's overtime goal at the Vancouver Olympics, would be the most addictive substance on earth if it didn't gum up the crack pipe. Any other country with a treasure this precious would guard the name Nanaimo (derived from the Salish for "too many traffic lights") as jealously as the French guard "champagne" and the Scots claim exclusivity over "Scotch."

CBC Radio once aired a show in which a foodie asserted that there are only two true Canadian confections: the Nanaimo bar and the butter tart. The foodie also claimed you can even tell which church bake sale the butter tarts come from: Catholic tarts are dark and deep, Anglican tarts are crusty, and the United

Church ones kind of shallow and flaky. (Personally, I'm terribly offended by this remark and think anyone who is upset should complain to CBC Radio—or at least not me—c/o Your Tax Dollars at Work, 666 Satan Place, Godless, ON.)

CRIME

Americans sometimes think of Canada as a non-violent utopia where peace and tranquility reign—sort of like Woodstock without the brown acid.

Alas, this image is not supported by the evidence. A cursory glance at the hockey highlights will show that we like our violence, a lot. We once had a prime minister, Jean Chrétien, whose popularity was based solely on his willingness to throttle his own protesters. Historically, we like to get a two-year head start on the US when fighting world wars.

What we don't do is shoot each other, at least not at the same rate as you guys. The US murder rate is three times that of Canada, and the gun-crime rate is seven times higher. (More than thirty thousand gun deaths a year, and what does the US ban? Lawn darts and Kinder Surprise eggs. Not that we're criticizing your gun laws, Tex. Ease it back into the holster, big fella. Ease it back . . .)

Really, we're no less homicidal than you. It's just that without guns, we have to chase our victims on foot, which is hard to do in a snowmobile suit. By the time we finally catch them, we're out of breath, have to take a knee, and call time out. Which is why Americans get life for murder, but Canadians get five minutes for high-sticking.

POLITICS

Visitors will recognize our parliamentary system of government as being similar to that of Great Britain, only without the fox hunts and sex scandals. Federally, Canada is governed by the Liberals, a party that for a century and a half has been committed to a single guiding principle: clinging to power like it's the last life raft on the *Titanic*. (Note: British Columbia is governed by a similarly named party, though they aren't so much liberals as unarmed Republicans.)

The federal Liberals are led by a man named Trudeau the Younger. He's the one who stopped you in the airport to pose for a selfie. Don't worry. He does that with everybody.

The Liberals took over from the Conservatives, who—unlike the Liberals—are highly principled and can claim nationwide support for their deeply entrenched beliefs.

Unfortunately for the Conservatives, the nation in question is Saudi Arabia, and the beliefs are those of the nineteenth century. Conservatives are unshakable in their support for the rights of individuals, except for immigrants, Aboriginals, enviros, and maybe the French. Put another way, they are 110 percent behind minority rights, as long as they conform to the wishes of the majority.

Also in the mix is the New Democratic Party. It's an odd name, considering there never was an Old Democratic Party, just as there never was a band named the Old Kids on the Block.

New Democrats also espouse individual freedom, as long as it doesn't involve the freedom to buy medical care when you need it.

What they really believe in is social engineering through government regulation: smoking bans, watering restrictions, mandatory composting, and equal access to the ten-month waiting list at the prenatal clinic.

GOVERNMENT

Canada loves its officialdom. We believe in government the way Americans believe in freedom. You have wars, we have royal commissions. It's a function of history: the US won its liberty through bloody revolution, while Canada just sort of grew up and left home after high school.

Your Declaration of Independence celebrated individual choice—"Life, Liberty, and the Pursuit of Happiness"—while our constitution, promising "Peace, Order, and good Government," nestled us safely in the arms of Big Brother. And Canada truly is a peaceful and orderly nation, if by "peaceful and orderly" you mean Jack Nicholson after the lobotomy in *One Flew over the Cuckoo's Nest*.

We are a compliant lot. Our national animal is a beaver, but might as well be a sheep. (Old joke—Q: How do you get twenty Canadians out of a pool? A: Ask them to leave.)

Alas, our docile nature leaves us mute in the face of non-sensical bureaucracy. As a nation, we allow airline passengers to carry 3.4 ounces of pudding as carry-on luggage, but not 3.5. Here in Victoria, we have at times passed bylaws banning bongo drums, sidewalk mascots, and the sale of balloon animals. None of this is questioned.

In our defence, we should note that Canadians are wild-eyed, live-free-or-die libertarians compared to the technocrats of the European Union, home to all those legendary butter mountains, wine lakes, and other agri-geographical phenomena growing out of a Byzantine matrix of farm subsidies.

And in defence of red tape, it should also be noted that many would-be retirees might not be working on the Freedom 85 plan—you can find them working the cash register at Subway, leaning on their walkers—had the US financial markets seen a little more regulation and a little less Enron, Bernie Madoff, and subprime shenanigans.

THE METRIC SYSTEM

You may have noticed that some Canadians speak to you in two languages. No, not French and English, but imperial and metric.

Canada, being much more culturally sophisticated and globally integrated than the United States, officially went metric more than four decades ago. This is why Canadians don't think it odd that they buy butter not by the pound, but in 454-gram packages.

It was in 1970 that Canada announced it would adopt the *Système international d'unités* (literal translation: *Pierre Trudeau Is a Draft-Dodging Pinko*).

Back then, the only Canadians who understood the metric system were scientists, track athletes, and hashish dealers. It's much different today—dealers of a wide range of drugs now sell by the gram.

Visitors to Canada may be confused by what seems to be an uncertain commitment to metric conversion. Some items are measured in the new manner, some in the old. Restaurants offer litres of wine but pints of beer. Stores sell packaged goods in metric units, but fruit and vegetables go primarily by the pound.

Fabric retails by the metre, topsoil by the yard, and gasoline by the arm and leg.

Socket sets come in both imperial and metric, which makes repacking them a real treat when they spill all over the driveway. Lumberyards (metres?) still sell two-by-fours (which are actually 1½ by 3½ inches), but most plywood is millimetres thick.

Deli products are marketed by the hundred grams, because that sounds cheaper, while the meat department displays price-per-pound signs more prominently for the same reason. Television screens used to be sized in inches. Today, it's hectares.

As for people, they are measured in feet and pounds everywhere but on their driver's licences.

Canadians can offer visitors a logical explanation for all this ambiguity: we gave up. Not only that, but we gave up partway through the process, leaving the country with half a cat and half a dog.

Canadians may no longer translate weather or speed to imperial measure, but few know what a metric teaspoon looks like, or what a two-thousand-square-foot house is in gigajoules, or whatever.

Oh, it began well enough. Toothpaste went metric in 1974. In 1975, Fahrenheit was dropped in favour of Celsius. (This was the beginning of global warming.) By the end of 1977, all road signs were in kilometres, as were the speedometers of new cars. Most grocery scales converted by 1983.

But 1983 was also when the federal government announced a moratorium on the application of metric weights-and-measures regulations. In 1984, Brian Mulroney's Progressive Conservatives announced Ottawa would not prosecute violators of metric laws.

The Metric Commission of Canada disbanded in 1985, and was replaced by a small office within Industry Canada. This office was itself disbanded in 1988.

Today, Canada's metric system is overseen by a part-time summer student named Hank, though he's thinking of leaving for an assistant shift supervisor's job at Pizza Hut. Well, no, Measurement Canada still responds to complaints, but it's not the most fearsome arm of government.

Our ambivalence and uncertainty occasionally creates trouble. In 1983, an Air Canada Boeing 767 made an unscheduled, unpowered landing in Gimli, Manitoba, after running out of fuel at forty thousand feet—or, rather, fourteen hundred kilopascals—due to a metric conversion error. (At least the Gimli Glider fared better than NASA. In 1999, an American-to-metric mix-up caused a US$125 million spacecraft to disappear into Mars's atmosphere and, presumably, burn up.)

Newspapers are particularly guilty of toggling back and forth between systems or, worse, pedantically translating approximate measurements into precise ones. Hence the story out of Regina the other day, when a three-pound puppy in a sixteen-foot hole became a 1.35-kilogram dog that fell 4.8 metres.

Meanwhile, the official line is that Ottawa is leaving it to the marketplace to determine the pace of conversion. That should mean the process will be complete in a couple of centuries, or, as we say in Canada, three kilowatt hours.

HISTORY

Here's a brief history of the Great White North, as provided by Kenny, an intern we hired this summer based on his excellent multiplatform crowdsourced digital content generation skills, whatever that means:

The first known contact between Aboriginal Canadians and explorers from abroad came in 1000 BC when the Minnesota Vikings played an away game at L'Anse aux Meadows, Newfoundland.

Fearing this NFL invasion would lead to the demise of the Canadian Football League, Aboriginals sent the Vikings packing. It wasn't until 1497 that Europeans would return to Canadian shores in the person of English television actor Sebastian Cabot, who played Mr. French in the 1960s sitcom *Family Affair*.

French exploration continued with the arrival of Jacques Cartier, who established a chain of fur-trading posts and fine jewellery stores along the St. Lawrence River. It was Cartier who first heard the Huron-Iroquois word *Canada*, meaning "big pink bit on the map."

Western exploration and the fur trade were both soon taken over by the British in the form of the Hudson's Bay Company, though the latter soon found itself in a long, bitter struggle with such rivals as the North West Company and Canadian Tire, which provided the wheels for the Red River carts that became emblematic of Manitoba settlers.

Meanwhile, the western coast was reached in 1778 by Capt James Cook, who had set out across the Pacific "to boldly go where no man has gone before." Cook defeated both the Spanish (who gave us such place names as Cortes, Quadra, and Galiano Islands) and the Klingons, whose influence can still be felt on the rest of the Gulf Islands, which are about as spacey as it gets.

Confederation came on the Fourth of July, 1867, following the Charlottetown Conference in Quebec City, which was then known by its native name *Regina*, or "Pile of Bones." The first prime minister, Sir John A. Appleseed, opened up the West to farming by building a railroad that was completed when Pierre Berton drove the Last Spike in the Klondike, an event that lives on in Gordon Lightfoot's "The Wreck of the Edmund Fitzgerald." Alas, the Klondike was soon stripped of gold, just like Ben Johnson at the Seoul Olympics, leading to a national malaise known as the Great Depression.

The funk didn't lift until the assassination of Louis Riel sparked the First World War, where Canada came of age at Vimy Ridge but, lacking proper ID, was sent home without liquor. This was known as Prohibition.

The First World War was so successful that they held a sequel, just like *Wayne's World 2*, though the latter was a bigger bomb. Speaking of bombing, it wasn't until the Japanese attacked the domestic car market that the USA agreed to join Canada in the war on Germany, signing an agreement known as the Otto Pact. But this call to arms was ignored by Quebecers who, objecting to the air force's use of the Planes of Abraham, merely turned over in their beds and went back to sleep (the Quiet Revolution).

This highlighted the schism between French and English Canada, a rift that was only healed in 1984 when the two solitudes joined together in chucking Pierre Trudeau on the political dungheap (leading to his famous declaration "Just wash me").

Trudeau was replaced by Brian Mulroney, best known for bringing in the NAFTA agreement that sent Wayne Gretzky to the Los Angeles Kings in exchange for a softwood-lumber tariff.

We are now led by yet another Trudeau, the political equivalent of buying an iPhone 6. As with the iPhone, and as mentioned earlier (see "Politics," above), this next-gen Trudeau's primary function is to take selfies.

ADVENTURE TOURISM

Some people think the term *Canadian adventure tourism* is an oxymoron.

In fact, a United Nations report says Canada is missing out on a worldwide travel boom because international tourists think this country is too dull.

Who, us?

The birthplace of Anne Murray, televised curling, and *The Littlest Hobo*, dull? The home of revolution-by-referendum, cookie-cutter strip-mall architecture, and "World's Politest Rapper" Drake, boring?

Apparently so.

"We are finding that young people are driving the world tourism market, but the image Canada has might not appeal to them very much," said John Kester of the World Tourism Organization. "It's seen as quiet, safe. I don't think many people think of Canada as a very exciting destination."

Well, obviously this John Kester fellow has never experienced the thrill-ride adrenalin rush of Victoria's tourism trifecta— Butchart Gardens, tea at the Empress, cheap heart pills at the pharmacy—or tasted the delights of our city's nightlife (early-bird special at four thirty, late show begins at six forty-five, don't miss our New Year's Eve celebration from 7 to 9 p.m.)

Or perhaps he has.

Canada is, after all, the World Capital of Caution, the country of peanut-free schools, bright orange safety vests, January lawn-watering restrictions, and a founding constitution whose loftiest goal is "Peace, Order, and good Government." The same nation that once won the Battle of Vimy Ridge now requires liability waivers for school field trips to the museum.

Our media image doesn't help. The *New Republic* magazine proclaimed this to be the most boring headline imaginable spotted in print: "Worthwhile Canadian Initiative."

A comedian once referred to Canada as the designated driver of North America. It was an apt description. We're the responsible, dependable one, always staying within ten kilometres of the posted speed limit, never getting the car stuck in Iraq at 3 a.m. ("Canada? It's George Dubya Bush. Me and Tony Blair got the Camaro up to her axles in the sand and could really use a hand . . .")

As for you Americans, you tend to just see us as Green Bay, Wisconsin, without the Packers.

We were actually deemed intriguing for, oh, eight minutes back in 2003, when Canada said yes to same-sex marriage and medical marijuana, and no to the war in Iraq.

"Whoa! Canada!" was the headline on a piece in the *Washington Post*: "Just when you had all but forgotten that carbon-based life exists above the forty-ninth parallel, those sly Canadians have redefined their entire nation as Berkeley North." Britain's *Guardian* ran a similar piece titled "Canada Gets Interesting."

Which, when you think of it, is as backhanded a compliment as a country can receive. "Canada gets interesting" is the equivalent of "Germans relax," "Scots learn to cook," "Pigs fly," or something equally unlikely.

In other words: Nice place to live, but you wouldn't want to visit there.

OUR NATIONAL ANTHEM

Please don't boo it.

Shouldn't have to say this, but every once in a while, we get in an anthem war.

This happens every few years. Usually it begins when some third-rate Las Vegas lounge singer inadvertently butchers the words to "O Canada" at a televised sporting event.

So then we Canadians, our national pride badly bruised, respond by (a) recalling our ambassador from Washington, and (b) booing "The Star-Spangled Banner" the next time a US-based team plays in Montreal.

This inspires American fans to not only boo "O Canada" the next time the Leafs are in town, but to drown it out by chanting "USA! USA!" in that annoying, three-beer-past-belligerent manner we have come to expect of those who confuse chauvinism with patriotism.

So Vancouver crowds retaliate by not only belting out our anthem, but doing so in the original French, just to show how cool we are: *Ô Canada! Terre de nos aïeux / Ton front est ceint de fleurons glorieux / Car ton bras sait porter l'épée, / Il sait porter la croix!* (Translation: "O Canada! Land of our forefathers / Thy brow is wreathed with a glorious garland of flowers. / Hey, let's go downtown and torch some cop cars.")

Then we puff out our chests and congratulate each other, because self-righteous anti-Americanism is the last socially acceptable form of bigotry.

This brings us to our next topic:

SMUG ANTI-AMERICANISM

I once referred in print to Stephen Harper as "an American trapped in a Canadian's body."

It wasn't meant as a shot (okay, maybe it was). The point I was really trying to make was that his beliefs were more in line with American values than Canadian ones. Readers, however, saw it as a low blow—automatically assuming it an insult to call a Canadian *American*, in the same way it would be insulting to confuse an 1865 Chateau Lafite with a nine-dollar bottle of Kelowna Paint Stripper. That assumption itself betrayed a core Canadian belief: we think we're better than you.

America bashing is as Canadian as hockey, Mackintosh's Toffee, or cheating on cross-border shopping limits. We tsk-tsk at America's gun laws, rage against your trade practices, sneer at your mawkish, bellicose version of patriotism, chortle at your ignorance of the world beyond your borders, and recoil in horror every time Donald Trump opens his mouth. (Let's not even mention your beer.) In short, we treat you Americans the way the French treat . . . well, everybody.

We do not (for once!) apologize for this, as we argue that it's David's prerogative to cast stones at Goliath.

Hence, no one blinked one Canada Day when *Maclean's* magazine published a just-joking-sort-of story listing ninety-nine ways in which Canada was not just great, but better than the US. Among the findings: Our annual health-care costs are lower (US$4,445 per person here versus US$8,233 there), fewer of us are obese (24.2 percent versus 35.9), and fewer of our politicians have been assassinated (three versus forty-four).

Still, there's a lot about the US we love. Only the most mean-spirited, ill-tempered Canadian, or perhaps an Albertan— sorry, I'm repeating myself—could despise the home of Homer Simpson, Disneyland, the Seattle Seahawks, *Modern Family*, and Ben & Jerry's ice cream. To sneer at America is to sneer at Aretha Franklin, Tom Hanks, James Taylor, and Jennifer Lawrence. I'm sorry, but if you sneer at the adorable Ms. Lawrence, then I am going to have to ask you to step outside.

Also, as individuals, Americans are legendary for being as open, generous, and friendly as a golden retriever, albeit one with an itchy trigger paw. (Sit, boy, sit.)

Nonetheless, we Canadians like to affect an air of superiority—just as every other bigot does, too.

The thing is, for a people who constantly exhibit a smug disdain for our neighbours, we spend a lot of time worrying about what they think.

Good grief, every time Jimmy Fallon makes a Bieber joke, it's the lead item on the Canadian networks' morning shows. And when Americans ignore us, we pout like a teenage boy who can't get the attention of the girl he pretends to ignore. (We tried not to be hurt when, one after another, all the US news outlets shut their Ottawa bureaus, beating a retreat like party guests who, one by one, glanced at their watches, faked a yawn, and went home early, leaving Canada with a platter of uneaten chicken wings, a cooler of unopened beer, and the sneaking suspicion that the neighbours find us, well, dull.)

Really, every time it's made plain that Canada is as invisible and irrelevant to the average American as, well, Greenland is to us, we turn into Glenn Close's psycho jilted lover in *Fatal Attraction*: "I'm not gonna be ignored." Next thing you know, the US will find its pet bunny simmering on the stove.

Anyway, you're here now, so allow me to once again say welcome/*bienvenue* to you, our American neighbours, and thank/*merci* you for choosing to spend your time/*dolleurs* here. Remember to do up your seatbelts and hide your handguns under the seat.

That's it. Enjoy your stay, but remember to drive in metric. To convert from miles per hour, simply multiply by a ratio of eight to five, factor in a large double-double, and add 5 percent for GST.

FALLING FOR
THE BAD BOY NEXT DOOR

Canada sidled up and slipped into a vacant chair at my table. "Is he looking at me?"

"Who?"

"The United States," she said, tossing her wheat-coloured hair. "He's sitting right next to us."

"I dunno," I replied. "He seems kind of self-absorbed to me. Why don't you look for yourself?"

"No!" she blurted, flushing pink, just like on the map. "I don't like him anyway. All that flag-waving, gun-shooting, tough-guy routine. Who cares what he thinks?"

"That's probably a good attitude," I said, tucking into my cheesecake.

"He's not paying any attention to me, is he? Who's he with, his 'best friend' Britain? The moron can't even remember that I'm his biggest trading partner."

"Er, I think he's alone."

"I bet he's staring at that tramp Mexico. Look at her posing over there, all hot beaches and cheap labour. YOU'VE GOT LOUSY ENVIRONMENTAL STANDARDS, YOU SKANK!"

"Sit down," I admonished her. "People are watching."

"The United States? Is the US watching? I shouldn't have worn this parka. I look like Anne Murray."

"He's watching you, all right. He's booing your national anthem."

"What!? Who does he think he is, the Parti Québécois? God, I hate the US. Always acting so superior, telling everybody else what to do. Why would he boo my anthem?"

"Hockey. It's the playoffs. Boston and Montreal."

"Arrgh! Is that all he sees in me? Hockey? All these years together, and he doesn't have a clue. I feel so stupid. Give me some of your cheesecake."

"Um, he said you had a nice personality."

"Great. Miss Congeniality. Why not just shoot me instead? I can hear him: 'Oh, Canada, she's so polite. Oh, Canada, she's so snowy white.' YOU KNOW NOTHING ABOUT ME, YOU DORK! NOTHING!"

"You're making a scene."

"Look at all the nice things I gave him: Ryan Reynolds, Chris Hadfield, Justin Bieber, Neil Young. That's it, I want them all back. Well, maybe not the Biebs . . ."

"He gave you some nice things, too."

"Like what?"

"Continental security."

"Against who, Greenland? Nobody wants to attack me. They don't even know I'm alive. The US doesn't care about my security. He just doesn't want anyone sneaking into his house through my backyard."

I squirmed in my chair. "Well, he did say you have a soft underbelly."

"He what? No more cheesecake." She shoved back my plate.

"I think he meant it's too easy to get through your defences."

"He did, did he?" Her Arctic got even colder. "That's it, the missile-testing range is closed, bubba."

"I'm sure he meant nothing by it. All he wants is control over your military, trade, foreign, health, and immigration policies."

"I should paint 'Welcome' on my forehead and lie down on the porch."

"C'mon, the US admires you. Really. He said he values you for your energy."

"He did?" She softened, lowering her Canadian Shield. "Tell me more."

"Yeah, he likes your electricity, your . . . your natural gas."

"Ohmigawd, I shouldn't have eaten the broccoli."

"Why are you so wrapped up in what this guy thinks, anyway? It's like nothing counts unless he notices. You just about faint if he mentions you on *Ellen*. I bet you even fly his flag outside your hotels."

"No, I don't!" she protested, but her face turned bright red—and it wasn't even autumn.

"You're a typical teenage girl," I said. "You base your sense of self-worth on the approval of boys—or at least one boy in particular."

Her tears began to flow like Niagara Falls. Actually, it was Niagara Falls.

"I know," she wept. "I try to tell myself that his opinion doesn't matter. But he's so big and powerful, he's hard to ignore—not that he ever pays attention to me!"

"Are you sure that's what you want?" I asked. "Guys like the United States are really only interested in one thing . . ."

"Crippling the Canadian forest industry with unfair, blatantly protectionist softwood lumber duties?"

"Okay, they're interested in two things," I said. "And your well-being isn't one of them."

CANADA'S
HISTORY, BACKWARDS

I recorded a documentary on the history of Canada the other night. Came to the end and started watching it backwards. Here's what I learned.

Canada was born in 2016 as a flourishing, cosmopolitan, industrialized country with two official languages, 35 million people, and 159 million Roll-Up-the-Rim-to-Win cups.

It's difficult to believe that from such promising beginnings came the tumult, dissension, and decay that would later tear this nation apart.

Yet it didn't take long for the social upheaval to start. The collapse of oil prices in 2015 led to the economic meltdown of 2008, creating a breeding ground for the grasping Me Generation of the 1990s and '80s and the radicals of the 1970s and '60s. The prime minister was deposed in a popular uprising—Trudeaumania—in 1968, but this failed to stem the exodus of worried citizens. The population continued to decline. "Ca-na-da, now we are 20 million" lamented songwriter Bobby Gimby one year later.

In the 1950s, weary Canadians welcomed the return of stability. Life finally became ordered, prosperous—even dull.

Although people enjoyed the material trappings of well-being, there was an emptiness to this soulless, suburban existence. A general malaise set in. There was a decline in social values.

This gave birth to a generation of angry, restless young men who, casting off the shackles of domestic ennui, set off in search of adventure. It wasn't pretty. They laid waste to Europe, wreaking such destruction that the Germans were forced to rise up and drive them out.

Shamed by their defeat and lacking in confidence, the young men came home with their tails between their legs, moving about the country aimlessly, refusing to work, burdened by an unseen hand. This was called the Great Depression.

Eventually, prosperity returned, and with it a sense of environmental responsibility. Gas-guzzling automobiles were abandoned in favour of trains, bicycles, and horses. The Alberta oil sands were reclaimed. Clear-cuts were replanted. Pavement was ripped up.

Alas, as Canadians' spirits rose, so did their consumption of the same. The authorities brought in Prohibition, which, rather than fostering sobriety, stoked the fires of violence. Still seething after the defeat at the hands of the Germans, another generation of young men demanded a rematch. At least this time they confined the fighting to the trenches.

It was around this period that women, disgusted by the testosterone-driven political process, chose to stop voting. Indeed, millions of people, disillusioned by Canada's propensity for bellicosity, chose to move to Europe. With them gone, there was no need for a railroad, so they tore it up. Pierre Berton wept.

French-English tensions, never far from the surface, came to a head on July 1, 1867. Declaring "René Lévesque was right," Quebec seceded. In fact, the entire country broke apart in a manner that echoed the 1990s collapse of the Soviet Union.

Yet, like battling brothers who forget their quarrel when threatened by another family, Canadians joined ranks behind chocolate heiress Laura Secord and took on the Americans in the War of 1812. Taking a cue from the expulsion of Japanese-Canadians in the 1940s, the government subsequently deported a group of enemy aliens known as the United Empire Loyalists.

Spurred by a couple of legacies of the Trudeau years— official bilingualism, Katimavik—the French and English attempted a rapprochement, moving in together at Quebec City in 1759. Unfortunately, the English couldn't figure out what rapprochement meant and, fearing that it had something to do with eating horsemeat, decided to go back to Britain. The redcoats, led by General Bernard Wolfe, secretly gathered on the Plains of Abraham and snuck down the cliffs in the middle of the night, silently boarding their ships and making their getaway before the French knew they were gone.

Lonely without their English friends, the French hung on as long as they could. They tried to eke out a living by importing furs from the Paris fashion houses and selling them to the natives, but it didn't work out. Gradually their numbers dwindled.

By the 1500s, Jacques Cartier had launched a full-scale evacuation of Europeans. In a scene eerily reminiscent of the last helicopter leaving Saigon in 1975, John Cabot weighed anchor and set sail for the continent in 1497.

"Thank God they've gone," said the natives. "We thought they'd never leave."

(Copies of *Canada: A Backward People's History* may be obtained by sending inordinately large amounts of money to jknox@timescolonist.com. Allow six weeks for delivery, then try to find me if you can.)

GET A ROOM
(WITHOUT A WINDOW)

It being a warm and sunny day, I decided to spend my lunch hour strolling the postcard-pretty walking trail that winds along the Songhees side of Victoria's harbour.

Rounded a bend and stumbled across a well-dressed, attractive-looking couple of twentysomethings making out on a trailside bench.

Not just sneaking a quiet smooch, mind you, but really going at it, writhing and squirming like a pile of puppies. A full-throttle tonsil-tasting expedition, as it were. At one point I think I actually saw his tongue come out her ear, but my vision might have been compromised, as it's difficult to both look the other way and gawk in slack-jawed amazement.

I must admit I was momentarily transfixed, and after fifteen or twenty minutes of me being momentarily transfixed, the young couple awakened to my presence. The man came up for air, glared sullenly, and growled, "What are you lookin' at?"

This didn't seem the most appropriate of responses. First, I wanted to point out, he was hardly in a position to be sullen. Really, he seemed to be having a terrific time, as did she. If I were them, I would have been offering high-fives (assuming anyone had a free hand) to passersby.

Second, it's not as though I had intentionally interrupted their ardour. I hadn't stood on the end of the bench, whistling and stomping. Nor had I succumbed to the temptation to holler out helpful comments. ("Need a break there, fella?" or "Watch your back, lift with your legs.")

Third—and frankly, I thought this argument to be so obvious as to barely merit mention—this was a public place. A very public place. Not the sort of spot one would choose for the brushing of teeth or clipping of toenails, let alone a noon hour's worth of button-popping snogging.

I wanted to say all these things, but suddenly remembered I was Canadian, so merely blushed, murmured, "Oops, sorry, beg pardon," and shuffled away.

Which might have been the best response, anyway, seeing as my views on public displays of affection, if not actual procreation, have apparently been rendered old-fashioned. The world suddenly seems full of young lovers less interested in finding privacy than a flat surface.

As Exhibit A I wish to point to the Oak Bay Tea Party, where security staff were forced to uncouple a couple who got carried away in front of an audience of elderly strollers, cheering boaters, and sandcastle-building toddlers.

To repeat, this was at the Oak Bay Tea Party, an annual event normally as twee and chaste as the name implies. Oak Bay, for those unfamiliar with the area, is the leafy, refined, and affluent municipality that is separated from Victoria proper by what is euphemistically referred to as the Tweed Curtain. Its annual Tea Party makes Downton Abbey look like Animal House by comparison. Until now.

Then there was the story told by my old friend Doug Bond, the legendary Victoria street cop. He was patrolling downtown late one night when he saw a pedestrian staring up into the ironwork of the Johnson Street Bridge. "Uh-oh," said Bondo, "there's a jumper." Actually, it was a humper—two of them, in fact. The passionate pair could be seen vigorously copulating way, way,

way up as high as you can get on top of the (appropriately) blue structure. Craning his neck, the lawman immortalized himself by shouting, "Hey, haven't you two ever heard of safe sex? Get down here." They descended as ordered (they were, after all, Canadian), and he sent them on their way.

Perhaps it is the effect of the sea air. My newspaper once ran a story that touched upon the below-decks boffing that occasionally turns BC Ferries vessels into the Love Boat: "One deckhand spotted an older man making love to a younger woman in his car. When the deckhand tried to tell them their behaviour was not appropriate, the old man replied: 'Go away. This doesn't happen to me very often.'" I would like to think that those involved were not locals but visitors lured to Vancouver Island by Tourism Victoria's infamous "Your search for the perfect orgasm is over" ad campaign.

Alas, there is evidence that Victorians, too, have given in to their baser instincts. I got a call from a woman whose sixteen-year-old daughter, walking down Douglas Street around 10 p.m. on July 1, was treated to a unique piece of street theatre. There, testing the strength of the bus stop bench on the city's main drag, was a young couple—he with his pants around his ankles, she astride his lap—boinking away for all the world to see. And they say romance is dead.

This, the daughter pointed out to the mom, followed a famous Canada Day incident in which a naked couple went at it while pressed up against one of the front windows of the Empress hotel. It was an intentionally public performance, timed to give the massive Inner Harbour crowd of ten thousand or so an eyeful to rival the fireworks across the water. Onlookers were shocked, or perhaps jealous.

(Meanwhile, one floor below, the jazz combo that had been playing in the Empress that night had just gone onto a balcony for a break. For one brief, euphoric moment, the musicians thought the crowd's enthusiastic applause was for them.)

It wasn't the first time someone had polished the panes of a hotel in plain view. Ontario residents will be quick to note that way back in the 1990s, Toronto's SkyDome Hotel became notorious for the activities of couples providing off-field entertainment for Blue Jays fans in the adjoining ballpark, which some suggested renaming Exhibition Stadium. (Others preferred the ConDome.) Eventually, hotel guests were asked to sign an agreement requiring them to close the drapes before they opened their arms.

Which is all well and good for Toronto, the Sin-ter of the Universe, but really does seem beyond the pale for virginal Victoria, particularly in the iconic, august, and ivy-clad Empress, where guests are more likely to rattle teacups than windows.

"Perhaps it was on someone's bucket list," suggested the Empress manager of the day, after being apprised of the Canada Day episode by staff.

Indeed, it really didn't seem to surprise him, given the general level of debauchery now associated with July 1 in downtown Victoria. "It does seem that some people lose their inhibitions on Canada Day."

Ah yes, Victoria's Canada Day/*Fête du Régurgitation*, a local phenomenon in which young people show their love of country by getting drunk, throwing up on the cops, and attempting to punch out the Captain Cook statue on the Upper Causeway.

Not exactly sure when this tradition took hold, but somewhere along the line, we ended up with a July 1 celebration that has more to do with hormones than heritage.

Think of it as a maple-leafed Mardi Gras. Teenage girls who couldn't find Montreal on a map parade around wearing nothing but Canadian flags fashioned in such a way as to barely conceal everything from northern Ontario to Saskatchewan.

The guys strut about shirtless as though they had just killed a lion, not a six-pack, displaying their patriotism by bellowing, "Canada effing rocks!" or "Effing Canada rocks!" or, when syntax fails them, "Effing rocks Canada!" This is usually punctuated by thrusting an arm in the air and making the extended-index-and-pinky gesture most commonly associated with the Texas Longhorns football team, heavy metal bands, or, apparently, John Diefenbaker.

Sometimes, the drunk tank is so full that they have to use the cells at the courthouse, too. Sometimes the drunks even come to the cop shop on their own: one Canada Day, detectives having a late-night break on the balcony of the Caledonia Street police station at first tried to shoo away a Lake Cowichan man whom they spotted peeing in the front entrance flower beds, then arrested him after he challenged them to a fight.

"I haven't seen so many drunken kids in one place since I was a kid," one dad observed as we watched a purple-faced police chief order a flag-draped girl to descend from the aforementioned Captain Cook statue, upon which she sat shoulder-ride-style while texting. ("Yeah, yeah, gramps, in a minute," she said, while not looking up from her phone, causing all the young cops to turn away and hide their faces so that the chief wouldn't see them laughing.)

Okay, maybe the dad was right, and teenage drinking isn't new, but at least in the olden days, we had the good grace to chuck our cookies at a Trooper concert, not the celebration of the national ideal. As it is, the fireworks display features as many Technicolor explosions on the Inner Harbour pavement as in the air.

Gosh, I enjoy throwing up as much as the next fellow, but for the life of me I can't figure out how Victorians came to equate puking with patriotism. Nowhere do the history books depict Sir John A. chugging a Lucky while wearing a T-shirt reading "Virgins Converted While U Wait." (No, knowing Old Tomorrow—who actually represented Victoria in Parliament—it would have been Scotch.)

Okay, the mob scene has been getting progressively tamer recently. Arrests are down. It has been several years since the Victoria transit system's all-time worst day, July 1, 2011, when it was forced to take a record twenty-five barfed-in buses—Vomit Comets, in local parlance—off the road. Still, Victoria's Canada Day celebration looks a lot like the cast party for *Porky's*.

Why do we do it this way? Maybe we're taking our lead from Vancouver Island's best-known export, fabled partier Pamela Anderson. When it comes to unfettered, unabashed displays of sexuality, our Pam pretty much set the gold standard for a generation. (It was a point of Island pride that she went to one of the Comox Valley's two high schools, while Kim Cattrall of *Sex and the City* fame went to the other.) Pamela was a July 1 baby, born in Ladysmith in 1967—centennial year—making her the most all-Canadian girl ever.

Or maybe this is just what Victoria really is. Forget the tourist-poster image of tea and roses, of Old World reserve mixed with New Age serenity. Forget the idea of the City of Gardens being a buttoned-down, uptight, prim and proper community of (a) retirees, (b) bureaucrats, and (c) retired bureaucrats.

If a guy can't go for a lunchtime stroll without tripping over an open-air theatre production of *Debbie Does Dallas Road*, or can't play bridge without a safety net, then Victoria must be ready to lose its sense of decorum, as well as its pants.

But I don't think so. So if you're out in public and find yourself struck by the urge to swallow a tongue other than your own, please, get a room. Preferably in Vancouver.

A couple of treks through time...

THE LIBERATION OF DUNCAN: A BC DAY TEST

It's the BC Day long weekend, time to celebrate the anniversary of, um, what?

"The liberation of the town of Duncan," I told the American tourist who asked. "Drove out the Russians. Our king, Bobby Clarke, broke their king's ankle with a hockey stick. (We built a big replica of the stick, mounted it outside the Duncan hockey rink.) Probably saved Alaska from communism. You should thank us."

We're a little fuzzy on BC history. In school, they teach about the discovery of Newfoundland in September, reach the Plains of Abraham by Christmas, continue until the Riel Rebellion in June, then break for summer holidays. Everything west of the Rockies remains an unexplored blank, a mystery, like one of those maps that read "There be dragons here." Kind of embarrassing when the visitors ask for details of our past.

With that in mind, here are some notable dates in BC history to memorize:

- **1778**. Aboriginals and Europeans make contact as British explorers sail into Nootka Sound, are greeted by the Nuu-chah-nulth chief Maquinna. "They look harmless enough," says Maquinna. "What could go wrong?"

- **1793**. Crossing overland from Canada, explorer Alexander Mackenzie reaches the coast near Bella Coola (Spanish for "beautiful refrigerator"). Faced with a three-sailing wait and seventy-four-dollar fuel surcharge at the BC Ferries terminal, he turns around and goes back.

- **1805**. The Hudson's Bay Company establishes its first BC trading post at Hudson's Hope. The name of the town is later changed to Zellers' Hope before being taken over by Target—which, just as soon as it invades Canada, retreats to the US, leaving a ghost town.

- **1843**. HBC builds Fort Victoria, Vancouver Island's first gated community. Sir James Douglas is appointed president of the strata council.

- **1858**. The mainland colony of BC is established. So is the *Daily Colonist* newspaper, founded by a man who (a) changed his name from Bill Smith to Amor de Cosmos ("Lover of the Universe"), (b) was so afraid of electricity that he refused to ride streetcars, (c) picked fist fights in the street, and (d) died in madness. After that, Victoria's newspaper editors got quirky.

- **April 2, 1868**. Victoria becomes capital of the united colonies of BC and Vancouver Island. Conveniently located to the rest of the province, isn't it?

- **July 20, 1871**. BC enters Confederation.

- **July 21, 1871**. BC begins bitching about Ottawa.

- **November 7, 1885**. Lord Strathcona drives the Last Spike at Craigellachie, completing the Canadian Pacific Railway.

- **November 8, 1885.** Via Rail cancels passenger rail service on the CPR.

- **1894.** After having his pipe broken by a bullet at the Battle of Sevastopol, a French soldier invents the cigarette rolling paper, becomes patron saint of the Gulf Islands.

- **1931.** The Dirty Thirties. BC's Depression jobless rate reaches 31 percent, leading to the creation of the unemployment insurance system in 1941.

- **1942.** First "Whistler EI Ski Team" T-shirt printed.

- **July 30, 1962.** Opening of Rogers Pass completes Trans-Canada Highway, linking BC with Alberta.

- **July 31, 1962.** "@$&#% Alberta drivers!"

- **October 9, 1970.** Barry Wilkins scores the Vancouver Canucks' first-ever goal in a 3–1 loss to Los Angeles.

- **October 10, 1970.** Canucks miss playoffs for the first of forty-five consecutive seasons.

- **1972.** CBC airs first of 387 episodes of *The Beachcombers*, the greatest dramedy in Canadian broadcasting history. Kind of like being the hippest Osmond, but still cool. Quick, Jesse, call Relic!

- **1988.** Phrase "raw log exports" appears in newspapers for the first time. Government promises action.

- **1992.** Phrase "mental illness and addiction" appears in newspapers for the first time. Government promises action.

- **1995.** Phrase "BC Bud" appears in newspapers for the first time. Government promises action.

- **1996.** Phrase "leaky condo" appears in newspapers for the first time. Government promises action.

- **May 2003.** BC Ferries does away with its iconic/notorious Sunshine Breakfast. Nuclear plants must find new way to dispose of drums of Day-Glo yellow "Hollandaise sauce."

- **2016.** Sesquicentennial of the liberation of Duncan.

Feeling educated about BC now? You're welcome.

Now let's move to phase two, a multiple-choice quiz to test your knowledge of the province you are (a) moving to, or (b) fleeing as though it were on fire. Let's see how you do:

The 1925 Victoria Cougars were the last non-NHL team to win the Stanley Cup. After leaving Victoria, they became the
  a) Prince George Cougars
  b) Detroit Red Wings
  c) Quebec Nordiques
  d) Macon Whoopee
  Answer: Detroit. But the town of Macon, Georgia, had the best name in hockey.

Which of these is true?
  a) The first woman to do a full-frontal nude scene in legitimate film history was Victoria-born Nell Shipman in 1919's *Back to God's Country*.
  b) English-born Boris Karloff, who later played *Frankenstein*'s monster, began his acting career when he joined a touring theatre company in Kamloops.
  c) In 1957, the Academy Award for best animated short film went to Victoria-born Stephen Bosustow for the Mr. Magoo cartoon *Magoo's Puddle Jumper.* That same year, he became the only producer in history to receive all the Oscar nominations in a single category.
  d) Vancouver-born James Doohan—Scotty on *Star Trek*— was shot six times while landing on Juno Beach on D-Day. One of the rounds, all fired by another Canadian soldier, cost him his right middle finger.
  Answer: They're all true. For real.

Who was the last BC premier to be voted both in and out of office in a general election?
  a) Bill Vander Zalm
  b) Mike Harcourt

c) Glen Clark

d) Gordon Campbell

Answer: None of the above. The last premier both elected (1972) and defeated (1975) in a general election was Dave Barrett, forty years ago. The rest all bailed/were run out of town on a rail.

Bonus question: Should Christy Clark get a *Premier4Life!* tattoo?

The city of Victoria has more

a) Starbucks

b) Tim Hortons

c) McDonald's

d) Marijuana dispensaries

Answer: Thirty pot shops, fourteen Starbucks, eight Timmy's, three McDonald's. Insert your own punchline here.

The most popular competitive sport in Victoria is

a) Soccer

b) Hockey

c) Rugby

d) Lacrosse

Answer: Gardening

British Columbians' favourite pastime is

a) Watching hockey

b) Bragging that they don't watch hockey

c) Walking around with yoga mats

d) Fixating on real estate prices

Answer: Public shaming via social media

Their favourite social-media shaming subjects are

a) People who leave toddlers in cars (boo!)

b) People who leave pets in cars (angrier boo!)

c) People who throw cigarette butts out of their cars

d) Crappy drivers/parkers/cyclists/lawn waterers/people of Walmart

Answer: Facebook founder Mark Zuckerberg

BC joined Confederation in
   a) 1867
   b) 1871
   c) 2002 (1871, plus 7 percent provincial sales tax)
   d) 1970. Wait, no, that was the Canucks.
   Answer: A moment of weakness

The Victoria Day holiday was named for
   a) Victoria, capital of BC
   b) Queen Victoria
   c) Victoria Beckham, formerly Posh Spice
   d) Stockwell Day
   Answer: Who cares, it's a holiday.

When it snows, Victorians take
   a) A bus to work
   b) A plane to Puerto Vallarta
   c) A sick day
   d) Valium
   Answer: Valium

A true Victorian
   a) Thinks redheads are a visible minority
   b) Calls his 1968 Rambler "the new car"
   c) Wishes the police would spend less time on pot and more
      on Scotch broom
   d) Doesn't even notice a British accent, but thinks of French
      as a foreign language
   Answer: Liked the old one better

You are not a true Vancouver Islander if you
   a) Still notice the view
   b) Know what a block heater is for
   c) Are afraid of bull kelp on the beach
   d) Open an umbrella in a sou'easter
   Answer: Embrace change

If you sell a four-bedroom home in Edmonton, you can afford
a) A three-bedroom home in Sooke
b) A one-bedroom home in Victoria
c) Visiting privileges in Oak Bay
Answer: High tea at the Empress

Mount Douglas was named after
a) Sir James Douglas, the father of British Columbia
b) Tommy Douglas, the father of medicare and grandfather of Kiefer Sutherland
c) Muzz "Big Train" Douglas, first captain of the Canucks
d) Douglas Coupland, Vancouver author of *Generation X*
Answer: Sir Horace Mount, inventor of the horse

Winnipeg, Vancouver, Calgary, and Edmonton are
a) Canadian Football League teams
b) Warships based on the West Coast
c) Cities in Eastern Canada (everything beyond Salt Spring Island is Eastern Canada)
d) Jealous of Victoria
Answer: All of the above

The Vancouver Island marmot
a) Is threatened
b) Is endangered
c) Is extinct
d) Is worth chaining yourself to a logging truck for
Answer: Tastes like chicken

BC was discovered by
a) Capt James Cook aboard the *Resolution*
b) Capt James Kirk aboard the *Enterprise*
c) Louis Riel aboard a prairie schooner ("Ahoy, Metis!")
d) Frederick Banting and Charles Best (wait, no, that was insulin)
Answer: The people who were already here when the Europeans arrived

You are a true British Columbian when you can pronounce
a) Ucluelet
b) Tsawwassen
c) Haida Gwaii
Answer: Any of the above, and you can't say "Toronto" without gagging

Match the product to the price:

a) A pound of Dungeness crab	1)	$2,000
b) A pound of farmers' market organic whatever	2)	$2,000
	3)	$2,000
c) A pound of dope	4)	$2,000
d) Return ferry fare between Vancouver Island and the mainland		

Okay, as a bonus, let's try a few Canadian questions.

Which is higher?
a) Mount Robson
b) Mount Logan
c) The CN Tower
d) The Calgary Tower
Answer: The Gulf Islands

A Montreal-area mayor pictured with his hand on a Bible is
a) Taking the oath of office
b) Taking the Bible
c) Risking eternal damnation
Answer: Pleading not guilty

Canada's best-known scientist was
a) Michael Smith, Nobel Prize winner in chemistry
b) William Osler, the father of modern medicine
c) David Suzuki, inventor of the motorcycle
Answer: Burned as a witch by Stephen Harper

Match the quote with the prime minister:
- a) Wilfrid Laurier
- b) Pierre Trudeau
- c) Justin Trudeau
- d) William Lyon Mackenzie King

1) "It is Canada that shall fill the twentieth century."
2) "There's no place for the state in the bedrooms of the nation."
3) "Because it's 2015."
4) "Hakuna matata." Oops, my mistake. That's William Mackenzie *Lion* King.

Canada's most valuable export is
- a) Alberta bitumen
- b) BC Bud
- c) Céline Dion
- d) Justin Bieber

Answer: Beachcombers re-runs

We wish to apologize for
- a) Alberta bitumen
- b) BC Bud
- c) Céline Dion
- d) Justin Bieber

Answer: Beachcombers re-runs

Canada's first prime minister was
- a) Sir John A. Macdonald
- b) Sir Johnny McDonald
- c) Sir Lanny McDonald
- d) Sir Ronald McDonald

Answer: Drunk

The correct line in "O Canada" is
- a) The True North strong and free
- b) The True North strong and reasonably priced
- c) The True North strong enough for a man, but I like it, too
- d) The True North, now part of the US continental defence umbrella

Answer: The la-and of the free, and the home of the prudent

Canada's motto *A mari usque ad mare* means
  a) From sea to shining sea
  b) From horse to shining horse
  c) GST not included
  d) Roll up the rim to win
  Answer: American dollar taken at par

Bonus question: Why is Rex Murphy?

Bonus question number two: Was the Friendly Giant really a giant, or was Jerome just a small giraffe?

You are now a British Columbian. Feel free to start whining.

Unlike the tamed and populated east coast of Vancouver Island, the west side is a wild, isolated wilderness—and home to one of the most spectacular hiking trails on the planet.

This piece ran shortly after three friends and I stumbled down it in August 2001. For a real guide to hiking the West Coast Trail, I recommend Blisters and Bliss, *by David Foster and Wayne Aitken.*

THE **WEST COAST TRAIL**

Dear Diary,

I can't believe we're really going to hike the West Coast Trail! Months of planning and the adventure finally begins.

Originally hacked out of the bush as a telegraph route and means of carrying shipwreck victims to safety, the trail is now part of Pacific Rim National Park, winding seventy-five kilometres down the left coast of Vancouver Island from Bamfield in the north to Port Renfrew in the south.

They call it one of the most arduous hikes in North America, more gruelling even than the eighteenth hole at Olympic View, but I think they're just trying to scare us. Anyway, we should have little problem, as Norman Gidney, Peter Devries, Fred Hoppe, and I comprise a stout-hearted, level-headed group.

Day I

Well, we've taken the bus from Victoria to the Pachena Bay trailhead south of Bamfield, where we'll camp until tomorrow. Our packs are pretty heavy, about fifty pounds apiece. Fortunately, Parks Canada helped lighten the load when we registered this afternoon. There was the seventy-dollar trail-use permit, plus twenty-five dollars to be ferried across Nitinat Narrows and the

Gordon River. That's on top of the twenty-five-dollar reservation fee paid three months ago.

Not that the fees are a deterrent: only fifty-two people—twenty-six at the north, twenty-six at the south—may embark on the trail each day between May 1 and September 30, and the quota gets filled faster than Bill Gates's bank account.

They made us watch a scary video when we registered. Predictable stuff: This trip is for experienced hikers only. Rains 120 inches a year. Watch for cougars and bears. Hang your food in trees. Dangerous surge channels can sweep you off the rocks. It could take days to reach you if you're hurt, and we'll only send help if bones are sticking out. Blah, blah, blah . . .

We're not worried. August is the driest month of the year, so trail conditions should be good.

Day 2

Good news! The tent fly didn't leak despite last night's downpour. Off we go, staggering into the rain. We encounter a handful of hikers straggling back after only one night out. Their sleeping bags got soaked when they were swept off their feet while trying to ford swollen Michigan Creek.

The northern end of the trail is the easiest. It's pretty flat, with plenty of boardwalks to follow. Mind you, when they say "boardwalk," they aren't talking Atlantic City. These are as treacherous and slippery as the guy who sold me my supposedly rainproof coat. I spent more time on my back than a White House intern.

Norm took a spectacular tumble down a cliff. He tore his rain cape, but repaired it with duct tape. Red Green would be proud.

Actually, duct tape proves surprisingly useful, patching tents, covering blisters. We meet a woman heading north whose soles have parted from the rest of her boots. They are bound in duct tape.

The rain lets up, and we see our first wildlife—gray whales put on a show. We stop at the campground at Tsocowis Creek, seventeen kilometres into the hike. There are more than a dozen campgrounds along the trail, usually nothing more than a spot of beach by a source of fresh water. Some have metal food lockers.

Most have outhouses, but bring your own toilet paper. Poor Pete saw his toilet roll fall in the chuck.

My back aches.

Day 3

Wow, that was some rain! We began hiking at 8:30 a.m., and the heavens opened at 8:31. Didn't let up all day. Only got three hours of hiking in before taking shelter in a rock cave on the beach by beautiful Tsusiat Falls. About twenty bedraggled hikers warmed by our roaring fire. Among them was a nuclear physicist from Sardinia who fed us Parmesan cheese (or was that a Parmesan physicist feeding us sardines?). I would have liked to talk to more of them, but spent the afternoon shivering in my sleeping bag.

Foreigners seem to outnumber Canadians. We encounter Germans, Dutch, Americans, Italians, Germans, Czechs, Brits, Germans, Japanese, and Germans.

As a rule, the farther hikers travel to get to the trail, the better prepared they are. Europeans have the best of everything: rain gear; ergonomically correct walking sticks; high-energy, low-weight dried food. Americans come well prepared: waterproof pack covers, gaiters, lightweight stoves. Albertans at least have good boots. Islanders show up in thirty-year-old $1.49 Day running shoes from Woodward's, carry a bookbag stuffed with vodka and Snickers bars, and spend a week bitching that no one remembered rolling papers.

Speaking of paper, the boys made quite a dent in our remaining roll today! Have to be more frugal if it's to last.

Day 4

The skies clear, revealing breathtaking scenery: massive fir, spruce, and cedar trees, crashing surf, stone arches carved by the sea, five gorgeous young women getting dressed in another cave, not that I noticed, dear.

Nature is good.

At Kilometre 33, we get ferried across Nitinat. It's hot, and a guy on the dock is selling ice-cold pop of varying strength. It's important to keep the fluids pouring in on the West Coast Trail. Most people use tablets to disinfect creek water, but they have a bitter taste. Fred brought a great little hand pump and filter, plus drink crystals for flavouring. Terrific idea. I'd hug him if he didn't smell so bad.

Huu-ay-aht, Pacheedaht, and Ditidaht guardians patrol the trail, keeping an eye out for trouble. A Ditidaht man strolls by in a pinstripe dress shirt, looking comfy as can be. Meanwhile, a trio of young Germans who look like they leapt straight out of the Mountain Equipment Co-op catalogue pant past in the other direction.

We spend the night at Cribs Creek. We're halfway there, which is good because we're starting to get on each other's nerves. Understandable, what with all the cuts, bruises, backaches, and blisters. Pete's feet are in pretty bad shape, which serves him right for using all that toilet paper today. Sixteen squares I counted, four over the agreed limit!

Day 5

Migawd but that was a hard day! Encountered our first ladders today, leading up to Carmanah lighthouse. Must have been sixty-odd rungs, straight up, which is a lot with a pack on your back.

Just down the beach is Chez Monique, the world's least probable and most appreciated restaurant. Heavy plastic and tarps wrapped around a log frame. Chocolate bars, soft drinks, film, chips—everything you need on the trail.

Park in a chair by a table in the sand, and tuck in to breakfast: cheeseburger, Fruitopia, and an orange cost $11.50. Worth every penny. Cheaper than BC Place. We don't say a word while stuffing our faces, which is an improvement over the incessant bickering.

We've been trying to walk the beach, but that damn Norman misread his tide table, and we were forced to cut inland short of Walbran Creek, where conditions get noticeably uglier. It's been muddy all along; now it's a swamp. The muck will suck the boots right off your feet. Forget staying dry. We just try to find solid footing—rock to root to log. The humidity is oppressive.

Tried to get to Cullite Creek, but ran out of gas two kilometres short after crossing the long suspension bridge to Logan.

Camp on rocky beach. Food running short, leading to nasty four-way argument. Resolve dispute by stealing Pete's portion while he's off using more toilet paper!! Still, can cut tension with a knife, which I keep close to hand. Sleep with one eye open.

Day 6

Bataan Death March had nothing on this. Start the day by climbing 2,335-rung set of ladders to the leg-breaking, pestilential bog laughingly referred to as a trail. Then—surprise!—more ladders than Home Hardware, one of them through a waterfall. Plus two more cable cars—metal baskets slung under clothesline-like contraptions to carry you across wider creeks and rivers.

Sun rarely penetrates rainforest, but it's like a sauna in here. Thigh high in muck. Hikers drown where they fall, and they fall often. It's just like First World War trenches, only all uphill.

No food, but we eat insects with every breath. (Found Norman hoarding a Mars bar! Only one possible response; if they find the body, we'll say a bear did it.) That bastard Pete used the last of the toilet paper; we have to resort to salal.

If we can only get to Thrasher Cove by nightfall, we can catch a boat to Port Renfrew, and I'll never have to see these three fools again.

Day 7

Disaster! They won't ferry hikers out at Thrasher Cove anymore. We'll have to lurch last six kilometres to Gordon River on our duct-taped feet.

Norman gone stark barking bonkers, bolted into forest. Can't find Fred; his footprints disappear off rocky sidehill. Hope his water pump okay. Keeping Pete in front—I think he wants to kill me, just like *Lord of the Flies*.

Find marker for Kilometre 74, hike two more hours, find marker for Kilometre 74b. Throat parched. Drank ink from pen . . . writing in diary with blood on end of knife. Can't go on. Sweet death please embrace me.

The horror! The horror!

I love these guys, man! We're at the bar at Port Renfrew, having caught the boat across Gordon River nine beer ago. Norm just ate enough halibut to start his own fishery crisis. Pete is in the bathroom, soaking his mangled feet in the sink. Fred is out in the parking lot, burning underwear.

We made it, which is more than we can say for the nine hikers evacuated during our week on the West Coast Trail. Turns out that scary video was for real. We knew they call this stretch of shoreline "the Graveyard of the Pacific," but we thought they were talking about the sixty-six ships that sank here, not us.

But we got to see whales, sea lions, otters, eagles, and those half-naked women. We got to go to sleep with the surf pounding in our ears, and wake up with sand in everything else. We met some wonderful people, and, in reality, not a cross word was shared between the four of us (that Valium does wonders).

Most of all, we got a terrific sense of accomplishment, which I hope to never feel again.

The Albertaliban and other threats to our security . . .

THE **ALBERTALIBAN**

Labour Day, an appropriate time to consider the differences
between BC and its hard-working neighbour in Eastern Canada . . .

We were almost asleep when the snap of the trap in the basement sent us scurrying downstairs.

She was the first to spot it, over by the camping gear, pinned by the metal bar that cracked its back when it went for the bait. "Oh, that's gross," she said. "It's all red-eyed and hairy. See the size of it?"

"It's a big one," I agreed. "Looks like an adult male."

She blanched, shuddered. "Is it really . . . ?"

"Yes," I said. "It's an Albertan."

"Are you sure?"

"White cowboy hat, Yosemite Sam belt buckle, can of Copenhagen chewing tobacco in the back pocket—yes, it's an Albertan, all right." For confirmation, I pulled out its wallet, flipped through the contents: sure enough, a picture of a pickup truck where the children should be.

"How did it get here?" she asked.

"Probably in a grain car," I said. "Or maybe it flew in on WestJet."

She wrinkled her nose. "What's that smell?"

"Rye whisky. Oil. Sweat. Success." Not so much of the latter lately, though, which would explain the sudden infestation. Alberta's economy had tumbled with oil prices. With the bloom off the wild rose, Albertans had begun migrating beyond their borders.

She peered more closely at the unmoving figure on the basement floor. "I feel sorry for it," she said. "They don't seem as nasty when they're not looking down their noses at you."

Which is like saying the Oilers are a good team when they're not losing. Albertans always look down their noses at left coasters. And British Columbians sneer right back. They're like a couple of distant cousins who are occasionally, and reluctantly, forced to share a table at a family reunion.

Alberta looks on BC with pious, judgemental contempt, as though it had just caught it dipping into the collection plate in church. British Columbia responds with a mixture of jealousy and disdain, peering over the fence as Alberta wipes out the meadow to build a mansion as massive and gauche as anything on the Las Vegas strip.

For generations, Alberta has been Confederation's favourite child—hard-working, rich, focused, but smugly self-righteous, too, mistaking its abundant, albeit unearned, petro-wealth as proof of superiority rather than as an accident of geography. Alberta is a libertarian, doesn't like government. Sings "O Canada" on Father's Day but is pretty sure Uncle Sam was its real dad. Thinks Stephen Harper is a communist. Drives a shiny new Humvee, which it uses to run down endangered species and environmentalists (which, in Alberta, are the same thing).

BC, on the other hand, is the family oddball, stuck in a room over the garage where it can crank up old Bob Marley tunes without bothering anybody but Alberta, who can hear the muffled music through the wall.

BC works just hard enough to go on stress leave. Regards its abundant, albeit diminished, natural splendour as proof of superiority rather than an accident of geography. Smokes medical marijuana and wants the government to pay. Drives a '78 Volvo with a kayak rack and still refers to it as "the new car." Boasts of a diet consisting entirely of "whole foods" (or, as Alberta calls it, "silage").

If this were a family reunion, Alberta would be the rich, surly uncle who shows up with an unfiltered Export 'A' in one hand and a bottle of Canadian Club in the other. The kind of guy who goes to bed after chores are done, then gets up at the crack of dawn to bulldoze something. Ask an Albertan to choose his favourite fruit and vegetable—he'll name pickled eggs and Spam. Or maybe deep-fried hippies.

BC, meanwhile, is the loose-limbed cousin who rolls out of bed at the crack of noon and runs 10K to the unemployment office. If he does have a job, he phones in sick when it snows. Heats his house with grow-op waste. Blames the weather on chemtrails. Confronted with a flat tire on his recumbent bicycle, his reaction is to write a letter to the editor or protest naked on the legislature lawn, demanding government do something about it.

From Alberta's vantage point, BC is an indolent, woolly-hatted, woolly-headed, granola-smoking, tree-hugging, pinko wastrel who spends most of his time chained to a bumper in protest against, well, everything. (This clapped-out cliché is non-sensical, of course—sometimes we snort our granola.)

BC, on the other hand, feels threatened as the Albertaliban tries to impose its brand of grim-faced fundamentalism on the good side of the Rockies. Follow our example, they tell us. Tighten your belts. Punch pipelines through the forest to the coast. Stop listening to Sarah McLachlan. Trade your Birkenstocks for burkas.

Let us be clear: our struggle is not with all Albertans, only with those humourless fanatics who invoke God's name to justify their brand of repressive conservatism. On second thought, maybe our struggle is with all Albertans.

How else do you explain a people whose idea of a good time is Commonwealth Stadium in November, whose sports cars are made by John Deere, who find spiritual fulfillment in a no-nonsense work ethic that makes the Swiss look like the aftermath of a Grateful Dead concert?

On and on it goes, stereotypes and insults lobbed back and forth over the mountains. What do you call an Albertan in a suit? The accused. What do you call a British Columbian in a suit? The deceased. An Albertan's lifelong dream is to die of back-breaking toil. A British Columbian's dream is to spend his life dreaming.

We have no sales tax, they brag. Nor do you have fun, we reply. Albertans have money leaking out their ears, yet always seem red-faced angry about something: Trudeau, the National Energy Program, Kyoto, the gun registry, another Trudeau . . . Even their cows are mad.

Albertans, on the other hand, can't understand what BC has to smile about, other than the beautiful scenery, the mild climate, and . . . okay, they do understand, but that never stopped them from crowing about the Alberta Advantage, all those jobs, high wages, and low taxes.

Low taxes? Of course they have low taxes. That's what you get when the school system only goes to Grade 3, the entire welfare budget is blown on one-way bus tickets to Vancouver, and the environmental-protection program consists of picking up the empties after Stampede Week. BC's biggest expense, meanwhile, is health care for retirees from Red Deer.

The contrasts continue. In BC, you can openly shoot heroin; in Alberta, it's whooping cranes. BC has Greenpeace, hot yoga, BC Bud, and David Suzuki. Alberta has the Wildrose party, cold winters, rye whisky, and, of course, the late, great Ralph Klein.

Klein, bless him, was satire gold, albeit one who rejected the way both he and his province were portrayed.

"The image many people have of today's Alberta is one of two major cities surrounded by a whole bunch of cowboys and roughnecks, or rednecks, and horses and pickup trucks and pump jacks," Klein once told Toronto's Empire Club of Canada. "There's much more to the province."

Sure, there's more: there are Sutters. Many, many Sutter brothers and their offspring, all playing in the NHL, all grimly working their tails off in a puritanical, humourless Albertan fashion. Still, the enduring image is one of Big Oil and big hats.

I have made something of a hobby out of exploiting these stereotypes over the years, poking fun at the narrow-minded al-Berta terrorists, urging a handgun ban in daycare centres, and comparing the provincial cabinet to the cast of *The Beverly Hillbillies*, filling the cee-ment pond with Texas tea.

For reasons I cannot fathom, these observations have caused some Albertans to turn red in the face, swallow their Copenhagen, and fire off letters to the editor WRITTEN ENTIRELY IN CAPITALS demanding an apology/testicle. One writer labelled me mean-spirited for pointing out that the phrase "drunken Albertan" was redundant, while another was miffed when I said Quebec banning smoking in bars was as unlikely as Alberta pulling the beer machines from elementary schools. Another disapproved of my suggested Tourism Alberta slogan: "Come for the mosquitoes, stay for the frostbite!"

This was a typical response:

"Is circulation so low at the comic book you work for that you have to vilify Albertans? From what I can see, the only thing the majority of people in Victoria are capable of is protest. Pick a subject, and the loons will come out of the woodwork.

"Just so you know, the major difference between Albertans and British Columbians is that Albertans actually get things done and British Columbians study a subject to death and then protest the result of the study. Your attempt at humour failed; an apology to your neighbours is in order."

Ignoring the fact that his observations were absolutely true, this is the best part of baiting people who have no funny bone: they rise to the bait. It helps to be separated by nine hundred kilometres (that's 560 miles, for those who only speak Albertan), several mountain ranges, and a moat. I'm not stupid. They have guns.

This, of course, is the perspective from BC, where the view is obscured by that mountain barrier (which, by the way, cost us a lot of money to build) and a certain resentment toward our more affluent neighbours to the east.

Still, it takes the wilful employment of blind spots to perpetuate these stereotypes. Those who brand all Albertans rednecks forget that the province gave birth to Nellie McClung, Joni Mitchell, and BC's patron saint, Tommy Chong. Those who deride the West Coast's socialist ways conveniently skip over the landslide election of the BC Liberals, who are really just Alberta Conservatives with better table manners.

Other inconvenient arguments worm their way in. British Columbians squirmed uncomfortably when Calgary forced its restaurants to severely limit the amount of trans fats in oils and sandwich spreads, becoming the first city in Canada to institute such health-conscious regulations.

Alberta also leapfrogged BC when it forbade smokers from lighting up within five metres of the entrances of public buildings and banned the sale of cigarettes in pharmacies.

This was not the way it was supposed to be. We're the certified-organic health nuts who treat every whiff of tobacco (though not marijuana) like a cloud of nerve gas. They're the Kentucky-fried libertarian rednecks: "You can have my cigarettes when you pry them from my cold, grease-stained fingers."

As if that weren't disconcerting enough, the people of Calgary—supposedly the most conservative city in Canada—elected a broad-minded, witty, Pride Parade–marshalling Muslim as their mayor. (To our American friends, that would be like the National Rifle Association electing Gandhi.) Vancouverites almost choked on their quinoa-compost smoothies.

Then Albertans went right off their nuts and (good heavens, it still feels strange to type this) ended forty-four years of Conservative rule and ELECTED A NEW DEMOCRAT GOVERNMENT. In related news, hell froze over, the earth began spinning in the other direction, and the Maple Leafs won the Stanley Cup. What's next, Harper doing stand-up at Yuk Yuk's while taking hits off a crack pipe?

Alberta, it seems, has forgotten its place. As Don Cherry will tell you, a good player knows his role. Sweethearts score. Tough guys fight. In Canada, Albertans are the grim-lipped, humourless grinders. BC is the team space case, gliding up and down the left wing, a million-dollar talent with ten cents' worth of ambition.

At the same time as Alberta had its identity crisis, the slump in energy prices hit it right where it hurts, square in the oil patch.

That narrowed the economic gap between the two provinces. No longer first class and steerage, we became just a couple of passengers sharing a lifeboat, buffeted by the storm.

If that's bad news for Alberta, it's worse for me. It's no fun taking the air out of a flat tire. Can't prick an uninflated balloon.

But why poke fun at Alberta at all? Because it's there. Because our northern neighbour, Yukon, is too small to pick on. Because the US, our only other neighbour, is too big (and comes with the threat of nuclear annihilation).

Because if Alberta were one of the Three Bears, it would be just right.

Down in our basement, she bent over and freed the still-breathing Albertan from the trap.

"What are you doing?" I asked.

"Letting it go," she replied. "All it wants to do is retire somewhere without a wind chill factor."

I took a deep breath. "Be careful," I said. "They don't always behave the way you expect them to."

News item: A terrorism expert says BC Ferries needs an armed officer on major routes to protect the vessels from attack.

BRAVELY FIGHTING THE WAR ON

TERROR (FROM AFAR)

I'm in a restaurant in the Inner Harbour one day when I hear this olive-skinned guy order his apple pie "Allah mode."

Well, we all know that's Islamic terrorist for "God is ice cream," a call to jihad, or niqab, or one of those frightening foreign words, so I jump him like we're on *Jerry Springer.*

"Get off—I'm an Italian tourist," he says.

Tourist, terrorist, tomayto, tomahto, it's all the same to me, I tell him. In a town so lily-white that the Irish are considered a visible minority, you look like Osama bin Laden. What's for sure is you won't be hijacking no ferry today, buddy.

Normally, I wouldn't be on my guard like that, but if terrorism experts see BC Ferries as Canada's soft underbelly, well, somebody has to step up and be the Ab Master. Can't be too careful now in our post-9/11 world. Or so they say, again and again.

Not sure what a terrorist would do on a BC Ferry, though. Budge in line at the cafeteria? Bring back the Sunshine Breakfast?

A determined hijacker could try ramming something, I suppose. Give 'er enough gas, and you might be able to take out that great little burger joint down by the dock on Pender Island. Hard to maintain the element of surprise chugging in at fourteen knots, though. Not sure ferry-based terrorism would pass any reasonable cost-benefit analysis.

No matter. Reason has never played a big role in the Fear Industry, which never met a bogeyman it couldn't keep at bay with a little help from the taxpayer. Or a lot of help from the taxpayer. First thing they did after 9/11 was slap on an airport fee and stick us in passport-application lineups that snaked outside and down the street like a Dirty Thirties soup kitchen column (in Victoria the queues were so long that applicants paid homeless guys to hold their place while they went to work). Automakers, dependent on components from both sides of the border, complained the extra red tape added $700 to the cost of a car. We have spent billions.

This is the legacy of 2001: Publicly funded paranoia. Security rules that are wildly disproportionate to the probability of attack. Government-sanctioned alarmism. Bureaucracy and regulation masquerading as action—but question it and you risk (a) a wide-eyed screed about the need for vigilance/hysteria, or (b) being hung by your thumbs.

Fear makes people magnify threats that might not exist at all. After the twin towers fell, Victorians fluttered about as though everything from the legislature to the Dairy Queen was not just a potential target, but a probable one. We assumed al Qaeda had a to-do list that lumped the #17 Cedar Hill bus in with the White House and Heathrow Airport.

It didn't help that, just like people who are so self-centred that they think the world is going to come to an end in their lifetime, Victorians assume their city is special enough to make any terrorist's Top Ten. Hence, the discovery of a handful of anthrax-laden letters in the US spurred evacuations on Vancouver Island—the premier's office, a building at the Esquimalt naval base, the Salt Spring ferry—whenever an unexplained white powder was found. For real.

So-called experts only stoke the fires. We have been warned, at various times, that airports, ships, military bases, government buildings, hospitals, power plants, and pipelines are all vulnerable to terrorists. So, for that matter, are Pizza Hut, Crazy Bob's Car Corral, and those shuttles that run seniors to the casino. Our fears are only limited by our imaginations.

A few years ago, a Canadian Senate committee singled out Victoria seaplane and helicopter operations as "glaring examples of security neglect" and warned that Canada's ports are vulnerable to terrorists smuggling in "chemical, biological, radiological, nuclear, or explosive devices designed to lay waste to a large Canadian or US target."

Inexplicably, the Senate committee somehow missed the potential for a committed jihadist with really strong legs to use our pedicabs to sow terror, or at least slow traffic, on the streets of Victoria. Also, one of the fishing charter guys looks shifty to me.

Anyhow, the upshot has been the introduction of fees and procedures that turn even the shortest of journeys into a bank-busting, all-day affair that starts with a bleary-eyed 4:30 a.m. drive to the airport. Once there, you might have to pull off your shoes (thanks to Richard Reid, the Shoe Bomber who tried to blow up a Paris–Miami flight in December 2001) or have your Starbucks seized (thanks to the Brits who tried to use liquids in containers to blow up flights in 2006). You also face (a) being patted down in a way that should be followed by a cigarette and a marriage proposal, or (b) the kind of probing normally associated with alien abduction.

This we accept meekly, just as we meekly accept rules that prohibit us from stuffing our carry-on luggage with, for example, maple syrup, yogurt, or aerosol cheese strings. Whips are allowed as cabin baggage, but lacrosse sticks are not. Small snow globes, yes, big snow globes, no. Fishing poles are okay, sans hooks, but ski poles and bowling balls are no longer allowed. Drill bits and pool cues are verboten, while knitting needles and corkscrews are okay (as, oddly enough, are lawn darts, though presumably not the metal ones whose sale has been banned in Canada since 1989).

Why do passengers roll over and take this? Because this is Canada, the ultimate nanny state, where we never met a risk, real or imagined, that couldn't be neutralized through regulation. Credit our unique blend of fraidy-cats, insurance lawyers, and bureaucrats, but you can't even stroll the beach anymore without wearing a bike helmet, Day-Glo vest, and steel-toed sandals.

Ours has long been recognized as a cautious country. ("Canadians are warm, polite, hospitable and bend-over-backwards helpful," read a recent *Yorkshire Evening Post* travel feature. "They're also safety conscious to a fault." The story then went on to describe all the bear/cougar/tsunami warnings affixed to a hotel room door in Tofino.)

But now we in the Great White-Knuckled North have become not only fussy but illogical, our fears disproportionate to actual risks.

Canadians have lost the ability to distinguish between possibility and probability, and to respond in kind. We freaked out when SARS killed forty-four Canadians, but we yawn at the flu, which claims up to eight thousand annually. Heart disease does in forty-eight thousand of us every year, yet it's an Ebola outbreak in far-off Africa that has us shaking under our beds.

Parents are afraid to let their children walk to school for fear of some non-existent bogeyman, when the real danger is that the sedentary little porker is going to end up in a mobility scooter by age eleven, having grown up all breast meat and no legs, like a battery chicken.

It isn't just a Canadian thing, of course. In the US, Christie Barnes, author of *The Paranoid Parents Guide*, found the top five worries of parents are kidnapping, school snipers, terrorists, dangerous strangers, and drugs, where the statistical reality is that children were most at risk from car crashes and other causes.

The statistics don't lie: terrorism won't kill you; texting while driving will kill you.

Now, you might argue—with reason—that it is the Americans who have forced us to adopt the new security regime. Put simply, they don't trust us. US politicians paint Canada as a hotbed of hotheads.

They can point to a bizarre plot by a bizarre couple to plant bombs outside the legislature on Canada Day, 2013, and—more important to Americans—to the Millennium Bomber, Ahmed Ressam, who planned to blow up Los Angeles International Airport on New Year's Eve, 1999. Ressam was caught by Diana Dean, a sweet-natured US customs inspector in Port Angeles, Washington, as he came off the *Coho* ferry from Victoria with a mess of explosives hidden in the spare tire well of his rented Chrysler.

They can also point out that Vancouver Island enjoys a proud (?) history as a smugglers' paradise. According to newspaper stories, this goes back to 1890 when the US Treasury Department sent an agent to Victoria to try to infiltrate an opium-smuggling ring.

It was after the US brought in Prohibition in 1920 that entrepreneurs really hit the jackpot. The stretch of Victoria shoreline known as Smugglers Cove comes by its name honestly (or dishonestly). Rum-runners like Johnny Schnarr, who made four hundred trips from Victoria to the US, some in fast boats powered by aircraft engines, became minor legends.

Later it was BC Bud, not booze, going south, the common image being small boats zipping across Juan de Fuca Strait—less than twenty kilometres wide in places—with hockey bags stuffed with marijuana. ("It's always hockey bags," the Victoria-raised cop in charge of the Olympic Peninsula's narcotics squad once told me. "I could outfit the Canucks.")

The US border patrol has boosted its Canadian-border presence greatly in recent years, adding dozens of agents in the Olympic Peninsula and employing some mind-boggling technology. One story stands out: A border patrol agent, stationed with a radioactivity-sniffing device on the highway near Bellingham, chased down a car that sped past at more than 110 kilometres per hour. It turned out the car was carrying not a nuclear bomb, but a cat that had just received radiological treatment. Pause to consider that: they can now detect a radioactive cat doing 110 on the highway. The US takes its border security superseriously.

Still, it should be pointed out that when it comes to gunning down Americans, the current score is former vice-president Dick Cheney 1, Canadian-based terrorists 0.

Increasingly, we hear the argument that in flailing at shadows, in restricting ourselves in the name of safety, we harm no one but ourselves. "Experience should teach us to be most on guard to protect liberty when the government's purposes are beneficent," said US Supreme Court Justice Louis Brandeis, back in 1928. "The greatest dangers to liberty lurk in insidious encroachment by men of zeal, well-meaning but without understanding." (Of course, Mr. Justice Brandeis was then hauled off to Guantanamo Bay and waterboarded.)

The question now, after fifteen years of passport logjams, air-security surcharges, sniffer dogs, two-hour check-ins, no-fly lists, footwear gropings, shampoo bans, full-body scans, cavity searches, and all the other indignities now associated with international travel, is where to draw a line between security measures that are useful and effective, and those that are the result of us what-iffing ourselves into a terrified frenzy.

Contemplate this while I turn my attention to a fellow diner whom I just heard order his meal "Allah carte," which, as we all know, is terrorist code for "God is a wagon."

THE JOY OF FLIGHT

Flew on a passenger jet yesterday. Decided, for once, to listen to the flight attendant's instructions. This is what she said:

"Hello/*bonjour* and welcome/*bienvenue* to today's flight from Victoria/*Bureaucracy-sur-Mer* to San Francisco.

"Transport Canada regulations/*règles absurdes* require that I stand here with a waxen smile/*visage de l'espoir perdu*, looking like a street mime dancing the Macarena while a disembodied voice repeats safety announcements in both official languages, neither of which you will listen to.

"There are seven emergency exits, two at the front, two at the rear, two over the wings, and a special secret one known only to the cabin crew. Since you are not listening, we feel safe in revealing that. Look, I'm holding up a seatbelt!

"Toilet facilities are located at either end of the aircraft, though should you attempt to use them, I will block your path with a drinks cart and order you to your seat. Although bursting, you will meekly comply.

"By now, you may be regretting your decision not to have spent the extra fifteen dollars and pre-selected your seat in the days prior to your flight. Blatant extortion, you called it. So now, instead of flying with your loved ones, you are sardined between a sumo wrestler and the feverish, sweating, coughing guy who smuggled the infected monkey in *Outbreak*. Not since that junior high class on sexually transmitted diseases will you have spent so much time with your knees clamped so tightly together.

"You will also note that since we began charging for checked baggage, most passengers bring only carry-on luggage, flouting the rules by dragging in bags the size of a small child. (In fact, at one point during the flight, you will hear a muffled voice from the overhead compartment saying, 'Dad, open the zipper, I can't breathe.') Should stowage areas all be full, you may sit on your luggage for the duration of the flight.

"Shortly after takeoff, I will dispense tiny packets of Bits and Bites, for which you will be pathetically grateful. To open the packet, tear at the wrapper with your teeth until you crack an incisor, then stab the pouch with a Bic pen until it explodes like an IED, spraying your seatmates with salted shrapnel.

"Later, I will serve army surplus meals packaged for Desert Storm in 1991, which is why the napkin resembles a Kuwaiti flag. Tonight's menu options include chicken Kiev and Chef's Surprise/*La Viande Mysterieuse*. Sorry, we're out of chicken.

"We encourage you to enjoy our in-flight entertainment system by plugging in the complimentary earbuds whose sound quality is comparable to that of an old drive-in movie speaker immersed in a bathtub. Only channel nine will be audible. Channel nine will be in Hungarian.

"Today's movie is *Sound of Music II*: Von Trapped by Cyborgs, starring Arnold Schwarzenegger and Pia Zadora. Described as 'a journey of the heart' by *Ice Fishing Monthly* and 'ninety-four minutes long' by *Rolling Stone*, it is almost as engrossing as the airline magazine, which itself is the literary equivalent of Wonder Bread.

"Or, even though you're not much for alcohol, you might prefer to simply drink yourself into a coma—though be aware that on flights of more than four hours, Transport Canada requires that I rouse you from your precious slumber to repeat the same announcements that I'm making right now. Apparently they think that first how-to-use-a-seatbelt lesson might have gone in one ear and out the other. Transport Canada thinks you have the memory retention of a fruit fly.

"We ask that you remain in your seats after landing. Nonetheless, half your fellow passengers will leap into the aisle as soon as the wheels hit the tarmac, as though this will speed the debarkation process. These are the same people who start their cars the moment the *Queen of Asbestos* touches the ferry dock, except instead of choking on their exhaust, you'll have their butts in your ear for ten minutes—dancing cheek to cheek, as it were.

"Oh, and by the way, today's flight is being diverted to Gimli, Manitoba. Hope you packed a toque."

Time to give thanks for things that go bang in the night...

COUNTING OUR **BLESSINGS**

Dear God,

It's me, Jack.

Haven't spoken to You for a while. Being a busy middle-aged Canadian man like myself, You'll understand. Busy, busy, busy.

Anyway, it's Thanksgiving. Time to count my blessings. Tallied them up, realized I had six fewer than my pal Taffy. Ticked me right off.

Which is why I'm writing to You, God. Having taken the time to reflect on all the good things in life, I demand to know why I don't have more of them.

God, You know full well there are certain benefits to which Canadians feel inherently entitled: clean water, dirty hockey, a warm bed, the latest iGadget, whatever we want to eat whenever we want to eat it, RRSPs, Netflix, four-dollar coffees, extended health coverage, bicycles that cost more than the average Nicaraguan makes in a year.

Okay, I know You are God, not Santa Claus. Still, Canadians assume some things to be a birthright, not a gift: single malt Scotch, double Air Miles, air conditioning, on-time newspaper delivery, and freedom from oppression/liberation by anyone named Putin or Bush.

We also expect a two-car garage that isn't big enough, high-speed Internet, a low handicap, quilted toilet paper, warm-weather winter vacations, and a television the size of Rembrandt's *Night Watch*.

Others might be satisfied living in one of those countries where words like *democracy*, *gluten-free*, and *I want your badge number, officer* have no meaning, but here in the Great White, where we explode like Don Cherry stepping in dog crap when cell service disappears for a couple of hours, we assume a higher standard.

This is quantifiable.

The Reputation Institute says we are the most admired country in the world, based on our effectiveness governance, appealing environment, and advanced economy.

Were we happy about this?

No.

We pointed to a separate study, the UN's Human Development Index, which in the 1990s regularly rated Canada as the best country on earth but now sees us wallowing in ninth place. Imagine that, only ninth best out of 188.

Ninth place might seem acceptable if you come from one of those countries that end in *stan*, where the unit of currency is the goat, or where the median life expectancy is less than that of a fruit fly, but in Canada, which we know You love more than Thy other children, we expect better.

Likewise, there are indicators that my own quality of life is diminishing. The dishwasher broke. My phone is a BlackBerry that looks like it lost a hammer fight. My car has manual windows (what am I, Amish?). They spelled my name wrong on the cup at Starbucks. My new car has a Bluetooth device that will only speak to me in French, just like my mother-in-law.

I circled the grocery store parking lot FOUR TIMES, but only the handicapped spots were empty (those lucky handicapped people get everything). Then I got stuck in line forever at the checkout because everybody was doing her Thanksgiving shopping at the same time. I bet people who live in Niger (dead last in the Human Development Index) don't have to worry about long lines of overflowing grocery carts. My life is an unrelenting hell. Is this a test, God? What's next—boils?

But mustn't grumble. Better to keep a stiff upper lip (at least until the Botox wears off) and give thanks for what I have.

Here goes:

- I am thankful for my health.
- I am thankful for the food on my table.
- I am thankful for the food on my shirt (sorry, dear).
- I am thankful for Thanksgiving dinner with heaps of dark turkey meat, extra helpings of fat-soaked stuffing, lashings of rich, thick gravy, mountains of mashed potatoes with butter, and pie à la mode for dessert.
- I am thankful for our excellent cardiologists.
- I am thankful that this year I finally realized my dream of being in the movies. (YouTube counts as movies, right?)
- I am thankful that there was no YouTube when I was younger.
- I am thankful for people who buy $70,000 SUVs, then complain about the price of gas, for they make me feel relatively wise.
- I am thankful that even with a life expectancy of eighty-two years, we Canadians can convince ourselves that our health-care system is in crisis, and that we are hard done by. Feeling like a victim is good.
- I am thankful for income and property taxes, for they mean I have income and property to be taxed.
- But I will bitch about them anyway.
- I am thankful that I have the mind of a genius, even if it does take up a lot of room in the fridge.
- I am thankful for lazy Saturday mornings spent in bed with a cup of coffee and a good book.
- I am thankful that Sleep Country is open on Saturday mornings.

- I am thankful that there are people who know how to dismantle land mines, slaughter pigs, and deworm cattle.
- I am thankful that I am not among them.
- I am thankful for my lush, rich mane of hair, but wish I could remember which drawer it's in.
- I am thankful that after I made fun of the People for the Ethical Treatment of Animals, they responded by sending me a free Tofurky (for real).
- I wish it to be known that I am also willing to make fun of Seagram's, Apple, Qantas, and Porsche.
- I am thankful that I was able to earn a great fortune in the newspaper business. Too bad I earned it for Conrad Black.
- I am thankful for déjà vu.
- I am thankful for déjà vu.
- I am thankful that Thou created me in Thy image, God, though my wife wonders why Thou couldn't look more like Ryan Reynolds.
- I am thankful that You are all-seeing, God. Where are my car keys?
- I am thankful I live in a free country.
- I am thankful it wasn't one of the ones freed by George Bush.
- I am thankful for free speech, that I can describe the prime minister as a "pretty boy heir-head" without fear of retributi . . . Hello, who can this be, knocking on my door in the middle of the night? Eek! Arrgh! Thud.
- I am even more thankful for free doughnuts.
- I am thankful the Fox Network gave me the opportunity to appear on a major current affairs show last week.
- I am thankful my mother doesn't watch *Cops*.
- I am thankful for my Colin Firth–like charm and sex appeal.

- I am thankful for self-delusion.
- I am thankful for Jennifer Aniston, but wish she would leave me alone.
- Did I mention self-delusion?
- I am thankful for sunshine on a summer afternoon.
- I am thankful for moonshine on a summer afternoon.
- I am thankful they caught the Shoe Bomber in time, and am even grateful for the security staff who now check our footwear at airports.
- I am thankful he wasn't called the Underwear Bomber.
- I am thankful eggs come from chickens, not pit bulls, or else they'd cost $800 a dozen!
- I am thankful vitamin C comes from oranges, not tofu, or else I'd have scurvy.
- I am even thankful when my wife catches me drinking milk out of the jug, then sticking it back in the fridge. Funny running into her in 7-Eleven, though.
- I am thankful, when I gaze up at downtown Victoria's hanging baskets, that I live in the City of Gardens, but it makes me wonder how they decorate Toronto, alias Hogtown.
- I am thankful that I am not the Halifax, Nova Scotia, receptionist who must now answer the phone using the full name of the Immigrant Settlement and Integration Services agency, instead of the usual "ISIS, may I help you?"
- I am grateful that an intermittent split-second shriek reminds me when the batteries are low in my smoke detectors, particularly the forgotten one way up in the hardest-to-reach part of the vaulted ceiling.
- I am grateful that even last night, when I desperately needed to sleep, the split-second shriek was loud enough to jar me awake at 4:23 a.m., then keep me awake by going off at one-minute intervals.

- I am grateful that the police respond so quickly to reports of rifle fire in my neighbourhood, even at 4:31 a.m., though I wish they would be more understanding when you explain that the smoke detector "really had to die."

- I am thankful that if I find it too burdensome to live in the ninth-highest-ranked country on earth, I can move to Mozambique, the ninth-lowest, where four in five people earn less than two dollars a day and the average life expectancy is fifty-five.

- I am thankful my problems would look like blessings to others.

- I am thankful that my life is so good that all I have to complain about are the things that don't really matter.

But I will, anyway, because (a) were it not for a sense of entitlement, I'd have no sense at all; and (b) complaining is what we do, particularly here in one of the most beautiful, most comfortable, most affluent corners of one of most beautiful, most comfortable, most affluent countries of the world.

Note the emphasis on "one of."

The 2016 United Nations' *World Happiness Report*, which measured the well-being of 156 countries using indicators such as healthy life expectancy, social supports, and freedom from corruption, ranks Canada sixth overall, trailing Denmark, Switzerland, Iceland, Norway, and Finland.

The Paris-based Organization for Economic Cooperation and Development's Better Life Index, measuring everything from disposable income to housing, also ranks Canada sixth, behind only Australia, Sweden, Norway, Switzerland, and Denmark.

Britain's Legatum Institute also places us sixth—behind Norway, Switzerland, Denmark, New Zealand, and Sweden—on its Prosperity Index, which uses measures such as health, personal freedom, education, safety, and security.

Obviously, we have some catching up to do. Not to sound ungrateful, God, but You're going to have to do better.

A SAFE, SAD **HALLOWEEN**

It's quiet out there. Too quiet, as they say in the war movies.

Usually, by this time of year, it would sound like the opening of *Saving Private Ryan*: the rat-a-tat of small-arms fire, the screech of rockets, the window-rattling boom of something truly explosive.

Welcome to Halloween, British Columbia–style. The Second World War 2.0, if only for one week each October.

But no more. Fireworks have, finally, become hard to find.

Growing up in Kamloops, in the province's Interior, I never realized the combination of Halloween and fireworks was limited to BC. It came as something of a shock to realize the rest of the country didn't think it such a good idea to re-enact the Battle of Vimy Ridge on the same night we dress our children in vision-limiting costumes and send them into the blackness to ask strangers for candy.

Visiting cousins from Ontario would take one look at this combination and ask why we didn't make the kids run with scissors, too. Small children, darkness, liquor, and explosives. What could go wrong?

Trying to explain Halloween fireworks to other Canadians is like trying to explain hockey fights to a Swede.

The fireworks phenomenon is, you must admit, hard to justify. One year, BC Children's Hospital declared this province to be the "North American capital of fireworks injuries." In Canada, two-thirds of all such woundings occur right here in BC at Halloween.

But here's the counter-argument: blowing stuff up is fun.

A case in point is the time I almost took my dad's head off, back when I was maybe ten years old. By this point in his life, my dad's receding hairline was in full retreat, having left him with just a thin little growth atop his head. It wasn't even a full-fledged tuft, more like a collection of stray strands huddling together for warmth. It looked like one of those lonely stands of scrawny hemlock that loggers leave orphaned in the middle of clear-cuts, waiting to be flattened by the first winter storm. Still, my dad tended it lovingly in the manner of a gardener who had coaxed a reluctant rose out of a patch of barren soil.

By now you know what's coming, which is more than you could say for Dad, who strode around the corner of the house one Halloween night just as I launched a firecracker off the front porch. Good thing he had his head down and was moving at speed; otherwise, I might have put his eye out. As it was, the firecracker exploded directly over his head, in mid-air, just like that atomic bomb at Los Alamos, vaporizing everything in the desert below.

I think it might have deafened Dad, too, or momentarily shell-shocked him back to Sicily circa 1943, because I made it all the way to the far corner of the property before he finally caught me.

Had that hand not snagged my collar, I might have reached Toronto by now, been living under an assumed name. Alas, his grip was firm, and the smoke coming off his head was matched by the steam coming out of his ears. I tried to calm him down: "Hey, chrome dome, how come so glum?" This did not have the desired effect. Likewise, in retrospect, this little Sunday parable might not have been as instructive as I hoped.

In the end, the government of Canada responded to this incident by banning the sale of firecrackers. (Sorry, my fault.) Fireworks sales were restricted to the week before Halloween, and minors weren't allowed to buy them at all.

A little over a decade ago, some municipalities went a step further by ending the sale of single Roman candles, demanding they be sold only in "family packs" with other, lamer fireworks like the oh-so-promising but oh-so-disappointing Burning Schoolhouse.

Then, after the provincial government rejected a total fireworks prohibition (opting instead for a marketing campaign declaring BC to be "the best place on earth to live, work, and blow your ear off"), many cities responded by enacting bans of their own, anyway. As a result, Halloween no longer sounds like the Tet Offensive of 1968, the distant firecrackers mimicking small-arms fire, punctuated by the periodic boom of the heavy stuff taking out a garden shed.

Not that we can expect a totally silent night. Fireworks can still be bought legally here and there, and even those devices banned in Canada are, in any case, easy to smuggle from the US, where regulations are looser. (They give you an AK-47 for opening a chequing account down there; you think they're going to ban firecrackers?)

But overall, in BC, it's finally getting harder to find bang for your buck.

The result is that Halloween night has gone pretty tame compared to the old days. Few accidental maimings. Not much vandalism. No longer is handing out raisins and sunflower seeds—as opposed to candy—an invitation to an egging.

In fact, the pendulum has swung too far the other way. Parents who as children revelled in the dangerous freedom of Halloween are now pressured to remove any hint of risk and/or fun from the night.

Every October they are bombarded with guilt trips from officialdom:

"Small children should never carve pumpkins," declared a Health Canada warning. "Instead, let your child draw a face on the pumpkin."

Ottawa also suggested feeding kids "a snack or light dinner before they go out to help prevent them from munching while trick-or-treating."

There was also a suggestion to "avoid baggy, billowing skirts and cloaks that might brush against a candlelit jack-o'-lantern."

A hospital chimed in with "Try to finish trick-or-treating before dark" and "Consider hosting a Halloween party instead of sending kids trick-or-treating" and "Young children should not have gum, nuts, hard candies, seeds or other choking hazards."

Even the fire department added a stating-the-obvious warning to refrain from shooting fireworks at one another (though I could still hear echoes of my mother's voice: "What are you kids doing inside on a day like this? Get your guns and go to the dump").

And get this: schools have banned masks and scary costumes, saying students should wear "caring" outfits instead.

Okay, so I have some advice, too: stop letting hippies breed with bureaucrats.

Too late. Having banned fireworks and turned the distribution of homemade treats into a hanging offence, the Toddler Taliban has now succeeded in encasing children in bubble wrap.

When did Big Mother take over fright night? When did the only acceptable costume become a fire-retardant haz-mat suit with an orange safety cone for a hat and a pack of condoms stuffed in the back pocket?

Halloween is supposed to be a little scary. It's supposed to be about vaguely illicit thrills, whether from bad behaviour or bad food. But no, no, no, today's kids aren't allowed to live on the edge, at least not without a safety railing.

The irony, of course, is that the tighter adults make the straitjacket, the harder kids will squirm to get out.

No coincidence that all the overprotective coddling was paralleled by the rise in extreme sports, hold-my-beer-and-watch-this shows like *Jackass*, and the vicarious adventures offered by the likes of *Deadliest Catch* and *Ice Road Truckers*. Call it *danger porn*, a form of rebellion unique to the first generation forced to wear a bike helmet while being driven to school.

It's not much different from food porn, a direct backlash against the constant hectoring of health authorities warning against the epidemic of obesity.

When KFC's Double Down—bacon and cheese between two pieces of fried chicken—was introduced to Canada, it was marketed as the bad boy of the fast-food world.

And it was no coincidence that it was Las Vegas—Sin City—that saw the opening of a restaurant called the Heart Attack Grill, where you can order the Quadruple Bypass (a burger that includes two pounds of meat), Flatliner Fries cooked in lard, and a milkshake boasting the highest butterfat content in the world, all of it brought to your table by a busty server in a sexy nurse's uniform (if you're going to be incorrect, might as well do it right).

It's not as though youthful rebellion isn't predictable. There's not a smoker alive today who didn't know that it was stupid when lighting up for the very first time, but did so anyway. "Just Say No," urged Nancy Reagan when her husband ramped up the War on Drugs (we won that one, right?), and Young America responded by reaching for the rolling papers. A teenage addict once told me that it was a school police presentation that first piqued her interest in heroin.

The culture of overprotection has become pervasive. Children grow up without any sense of personal responsibility; anything not specifically proscribed is assumed to be safe. They live in a world of car seats, airbags, childproof caps, knee pads, Day-Glo vests, safety cones, liability waivers, best-before dates, Stranger Danger, and duck and cover. Can't ride in the back of a pickup truck, can't take peanut butter to school. Our playgrounds have been robbed of any apparatus that spins until you trap a limb/throw up/have fun. Canada officially became a nation of pinkly soft, jelly-spined wusses on April 29, 1997, the day that Craig MacTavish, the last player in the NHL to skate without a helmet, retired.

Meanwhile, as our children are encouraged to "enjoy" this safe, sad, neutered, and lobotomized faux Halloween, their elders have gone off their nuts, transforming the holiday into an excuse to indulge in the kind of wild, lascivious behaviour more normally associated with pagan orgies or old-timers softball tournaments.

The weekend before Halloween has become a gong show in fishnet stockings, a kids' event hijacked by adults wearing scantily clad fantasies. You, yourself, might have groggily awoken in a beer-stained bunny suit, wondering how you ended up in (a) a stranger's bed, (b) the stockroom at Costco, or (c) a boxcar bound for Moncton, NB.

Halloween Saturday has in many cities taken over as the biggest party date on the calendar. In fact, it's four times as busy as New Year's for Greater Victoria police departments.

And the costumes! When did government pass the law requiring women to dress like they're pole dancing at a peeler bar? A couple of years ago, newspapers reported that the most popular getups included the Sexy Breaking Bad—featuring an unzipped, miniskirted haz-mat suit—and the Sexy Duck Dynasty, with a tutu, stiletto heels, and thigh-highs to go with the camo vest and hat. Online retailer HalloweenCostumes.com offers not just your traditional naughty nurse, naughty French maid, naughty librarian, and naughty teacher, but a "sexy" line featuring more than thirteen hundred outfits ranging from the Miley Cyrus–inspired Twerky Teddy to the Sexy SWAT Sniper and a Sexy Deer outfit that includes an antlered headband and little white tail.

Forget pint-sized witches and goblins knocking on your door in search of Rice Krispie squares. Halloween has become an excuse to shed inhibitions (not to mention undergarments) and dive into the kind of bacchanalia that would make Charlie Sheen turn pink at the ears.

At least this is a national, or even international phenomenon, unlike BC's fireworks tradition. It would be strange were we the only ones getting a bang out of Halloween.

A visit to the Land beyond Starbucks . . .

THE **OTHER** ISLAND

"When you go home," Pauline Alfred said, "tell your wife *qwallayuw.*"

This was way up in Alert Bay, where Pauline taught the Kwak'wala language to kids at the Native school.

"Kwa-la-yu," I said, only butchering the pronunciation a little bit. "What's that mean?"

"It's a term of endearment," Pauline said. "It means 'you're my reason for being.' She'll swoon."

Awesome.

Except when Dr. Romance got home and tried it out, this is the reply he got: "Whatever."

Perhaps it lost something in the translation.

Or perhaps it was the distance. Northern Vancouver Island might be just a few hours away by car, but in some ways it's on the other side of the moon.

Most people in Victoria never travel up-Island (most consider anywhere beyond Costco a lawless frontier). Some Victorians don't believe there's anything north of the Malahat at all, suspect the area exists in legend only, just like Atlantis, Hogwarts, or Sooke.

Of the few who do venture out, almost none stray beyond the largely unbroken strip of paved, golf-coursed, and Tim Hortoned humanity that snakes up the east coast to the Comox Valley.

If they did, they would discover a whole other island out there, one where the bears show up when the skunk cabbage blooms, the eagles swarm thick as mosquitoes, and the language is filled with strange, arcane terms foreign to the urban tongue: *caulk boots, eulachon oil, calloused hands*, and *I can't get a cell phone signal*.

Call it the Land beyond Starbucks. There are no traffic lights north of Campbell River. No McDonald's. Not a lot of people, period.

The fall is a great time to visit. Indulge me, dear reader, as we go for a drive (and the odd ferry ride) up to the north end of the Island, out to the west coast and to the smaller islands beyond—and maybe meet some of those who made them special.

SALT SPRING ISLAND

WHERE—*Between Heaven and Hell (a.k.a. Victoria and Vancouver)*
POPULATION—*10,500*
CLAIM TO FAME—*Contrariness*

Okay, we'll start our trip not far from the city. Actually, rather than being rural, Salt Spring is more like Urban Lite.

If the rest of Canada dreams of retiring to Victoria, Victorians stuck rotting to death in their office cubicles dream of Salt Spring. The island is lovely, trippy, safe, and secluded, yet is within easy reach of the world, and has a hospital, schools, and a rich culture—more galleries and artists' studios than Surrey has drive-bys. You can't throw a dulcimer without hitting a musician.

You also can't go five minutes without stumbling into an argument, with one grey-beard furiously signing a petition in self-righteous indignation while another drives off in a huff (or, more likely, a Volkswagen Westfalia). The island is notoriously fractious.

Maybe it's because bucking convention is at the heart of the old counterculture. Maybe it's because the newish wave of wealthy retirees have a keen sense of entitlement. (The island is no longer just the bucolic 1970s sheep-batiking preserve of artists and farmers, where the horses were shod but the kids ran barefoot.) Maybe it's because Salt Spring, which singer Valdy famously referred to as a difference of opinion surrounded by water, is known for its lamb, not its sheep.

Logging, gentrification, vacation rentals—there's always something to fight about, even when there's not. BC Hydro found people in the Gulf Islands were fifteen times as likely as those in Vancouver to reject smart meters. Opponents of the aerial application of a biological pesticide once went into distress after being sprayed from above, only to discover that the poison was actually salt water dripping from navigation buoys being helicoptered from one side of the island to the other.

There's not even agreement on how to spell the island's name. Local usage tilts toward two words, though there's hardly unanimity. The newest phone book has sixty-two listings that begin with Salt Spring, but only thirteen for Saltspring, whose name derives from some natural brine pools (or is that brinepools) on the island's north end. Several years ago, Canada Post declared the one-word version must be used on mail, but backed down after a minor revolt.

The only thing residents agree on (other than their abhorrence of BC Ferries) is that outsiders shouldn't interfere in locals' business.

··

TOFINO

WHERE—*Edge of Eden*
POPULATION—*1,900 in winter, 1.2 billion in summer*
CLAIM TO FAME—*Most beautiful place/people on earth*

Last time I was in Tofino, I saw a woman doing yoga on Chesterman Beach. At least, I think it was yoga. Maybe she was just trying to scratch her shoulder blades.

Doesn't matter. Her motions were slow and fluid, and she looked lithe and hip and beautiful. All the women in Tofino are lithe and hip and beautiful. So, for that matter, are the men. Ditto for the dogs. Tofitians even look loose-limbed and serene while surfing.

The tourists? We try to act like we're from Tofino, too, but never quite pull it off. ("I'd like a large tai chi, miss." "I believe that's a chai tea, sir.")

Never mind, kick off your shoes, dig your toes into the sand, and wander the beach looking for—televisions?

Yes, those were among the finds of Barry Campbell, the king of the beachcombers. A former Pacific Rim National Park employee, his discoveries over four decades included televisions, skis, 345 glass fishing floats, and, in 1987, a message in a bottle from Katano Elementary School in Osaka, Japan. Dotted around his Tofino home were deck chairs, a snow shovel, and a laundry basket offered up by the ocean. A mannequin used by the US Coast Guard for rescue drills scared Barry and wife Barbara before they realized it was just a dummy in a survival suit. Among their discoveries were sleds, sheets of California redwood, brick-sized plastic emergency kits designed for shipwreck victims, and eighty to ninety Nike running shoes, part of a shipment of eighty thousand that were famously swept off a ship near Alaska in 1990.

Barry said you can actually sniff out a good beachcombing tide, one where the telltale odour of rotting seaweed and other flotsam is carried on the south winds hammering in from the open ocean. One night he picked up thirty-six Japanese fishing floats, but getting them meant leaping out of bed before midnight and hiking the entire twelve-kilometre length of Long Beach—both ways—in a driving rainstorm, burning out four sets of flashlight batteries in the process. For this is the brutal beachcombing truth: if you want glass balls, you need an iron will.

GOLD RIVER

WHERE—*The end of the road*
POPULATION—*1,200*
CLAIM TO FAME—*Luna the whale*

Gold River is one of those mill towns that no longer has a mill. Happily, it has (a) good fishing, (b) a golf course, (c) cheap housing, and (d) medical care, so retirees like it.

While wildlife abounds in the area, the town is best known for a single whale. Before his fatal (and lamentably predictable) encounter with a ship's propeller in 2006, Luna became famous as the orphaned orca who loved people.

Separated from his pod (just like E.T.) in 2001, Luna was more family dog than whale, eagerly making a beeline for every fishboat, pleasure craft, or kayak in Nootka Sound. Sometimes it wouldn't let boaters dock, would keep pushing them back to sea.

The day I first saw him in 2003, he blasted me with blowhole spray (it tasted like chicken) as I leaned over the side of the tied-up prawn boat against which he was rubbing.

The photographer Debra Brash got a great shot of Luna popping straight up out of the water to go nose to nose with a black Lab in a powerboat. We ran into him again later that day (almost literally) when he suddenly surfaced right where our float plane was about to land. The pilot, cursing, hauled back on the controls. Somewhere, a little girl screamed. Wait, no, it was me.

NOOTKA ISLAND

WHERE—*A boat ride away from Gold River (take a trip on the* Uchuck III—*it's fabulous)*
POPULATION—*One family, last time I was there*
CLAIM TO FAME—*History*

Nootka Island (to be precise: Yuquot, also known as Friendly Cove) is famous as the spot where Europeans, in the person of Capt James Cook, first set foot on BC soil in 1778.

It's also famous as the spot where a snarling match between Britain and Spain almost escalated into World War I (The Prequel) in 1789 (apparently the cove wasn't all that friendly).

It's less famous as the place where the locals reacted to a series of insults and injustices by wiping out twenty-five men aboard the trading ship *Boston* in 1803. Only two crew members survived, one being armourer John R. Jewitt, who was kept as a slave by the ranking Mowachaht chief, Maquinna, for a couple of years.

As the two hundredth anniversary of the clash approached, the Mowachaht/Muchalaht First Nation planned a Yuquot gathering at which a descendant of Jewitt was hosted by the current chief (also named Maquinna) and honoured with a native name.

"We're also planning a re-enactment, but we're short of white guys," one of the band members told me. "Want to volunteer?" He was kidding. I think.

Nootka Island is great for camping and hiking.

WOSS

WHERE—*A million miles from New York City*
POPULATION—*Well, there were four kids in the school last year*
CLAIM TO FAME—*Generosity*

In 2007, with the north Island in the grips of a forestry strike, nobody had any money. Yet when the rain-soaked cyclists of the Cops for Cancer Tour de Rock wobbled into tiny Woss during their thousand-kilometre ride, they were greeted by pickets whose On Strike signs had been replaced with ones urging support for the charity.

Down the road in strike-straitened Sayward, the heat in the mothballed community centre was turned on so the cyclists would have somewhere to sleep. Up in similarly hurting Port Alice, the locals stuffed the riders with seafood and packed the Legion for a Tour de Rock auction where the most fought-over item was a basket of sex toys.

The lesson: The tougher things get up-Island, the more people help.

Ain't going to forget that.

TELEGRAPH COVE

WHERE—*South of Port McNeill*
POPULATION—*20, plus several skeletons*
CLAIM TO FAME—*Finny, the world's best wedding present*

Tourists love Telegraph Cove and its rustic buildings clustered along the old waterfront boardwalk. It's the perfect jumping-off spot for whale-watching, which made it the perfect place to open the Whale Interpretive Centre, featuring a selection of pieced-together skeletons: orcas, minke whale, gray whale, dolphin, porpoise, sea lion . . .

So in 1999, when a cruise ship entered Vancouver Harbour with a twenty-metre fin whale—the world's second-largest mammal—impaled on its bow as roadkill, Mary Borrowman leapt into action. She had a tugboat drag the fifty-ton carcass up to Telegraph Cove, where she presented it to her new husband, Jim Borrowman, as a wedding gift.

She knew he would like it, as he had already reduced dozens of washed-up-dead marine mammals to their bones. The first, a bloated minke whale he recovered forty years ago, exploded in his face when he cut it open. Stinky Minke, they called it. He was lucky the dogs didn't roll on him.

Anyway, Finny's house-long, articulated skeleton hangs now from the ceiling. Mary was left with another challenge: living up to her wedding present to Jim. "It makes it difficult when it comes to birthdays and anniversaries," she said. "You can't just buy him a tie."

SOINTULA

WHERE—*Malcolm Island, a ferry ride from Port McNeill*
POPULATION—*576*
CLAIM TO FAME—*Turn-of-the-century Finnish hippies*

Sointula means "place of harmony" in Finnish, the language of the people who settled it as a utopian socialist society after fleeing Robert Dunsmuir's Vancouver Island coal mines in 1901.

The commune soon collapsed, but many of its values remained. It's a remarkably self-reliant, co-operative community where volunteers provide the services that people in cities like Vancouver (civic motto: Somebody Should Do Something about That) expect their taxes to cover. Basically, the Lions Club and Sointula Recreation Association are the closest thing to local government.

That makes Sointula similar to communities on most of the Gulf Islands, where everything from firefighting to building ball fields, running the waterworks, and staffing libraries is left to volunteers.

This does not prevent city dwellers—the ones with taxpayer-funded hospitals, transit systems, sewers, museums, rec centres, theatres, universities, and so on—from indignantly demanding an end to subsidized BC Ferries routes.

....

ALERT BAY

WHERE—*Cormorant Island, same ferry ride from Port McNeill*
POPULATION—*1,500*
CLAIM TO FAME—*Fighting back*

Back in 1921, when the Native potlatch was illegal (don't ask; it still doesn't make sense), a chief named Dan Cranmer hosted one of the traditional ceremonies on isolated Village Island, away (he thought) from prying eyes.

Alas, the secret got out, and forty-five people got busted, charged with such heinous crimes as making speeches, dancing, and giving gifts. Half were jailed, and half were freed on the condition that their tribes give up their potlatch paraphernalia—masks, whistles, headdresses, and so on. The confiscated items were supposed to be kept in trust, but ended up being scattered in museums and private collections around the world.

Over time, the Kwakwaka'wakw (say *Kwak-wak-ya-wak*) people began the painstaking process of getting their treasures back. They succeeded thanks to the dogged determination of people like the late Andrea Sanborn, the director of Alert Bay's wonderful U'mista Cultural Centre, where many of the artifacts are now found.

While most museums readily returned the items, one of the last holdouts was the British Museum, which was reluctant to surrender a mask (no surprise; if it gave up all its stolen stuff, the joint would be empty).

In the middle of this tug-of-war, Andrea decided to have some fun. She showed up at a meeting at the famed London institution with an empty Adidas bag.

"What's that for?" the perplexed museum boffins asked.

"I've come for the mask," she deadpanned, this short, middle-aged Native woman standing there with a carrier bag, having travelled all the way from Alert Bay.

The mask didn't come back in the Adidas bag, but it is now on display at the U'mista centre. You should go see it.

VILLAGE ISLAND

WHERE—*A two-hour boat ride from the middle of nowhere*
POPULATION—*At least one bear*
CLAIM TO FAME—*The scene of the crime*

I once boated to deserted Village Island—also known as 'Mimkwamlis—with the Kwakwaka'wakw chief Bill Cranmer (son of potlatch host Dan) and the photographer Brash.

Cranmer wanted to lead us to a fallen totem pole in the forest, but with a narrow window to beat the tide, we had to hurry down a forest trail—right up until a steaming fresh pile of bear scat brought us to a sudden halt. Cranmer turned to Brash: "You should go first."

Apparently the Kwakwaka'wakw have a gift for deadpan humour.

ECHO BAY

WHERE—*Gilford Island, Broughton Archipelago*
POPULATION—*Almost no one*
CLAIM TO FAME—*Almost every home is on floats*

In Echo Bay, the family car is a boat. There are no roads. The entire community clings to the shore like Tom Hanks in *Cast Away*.

People adapt to this. I once met an eleven-year-old girl who tied a sea star to a rope, then lowered it into the water to pull up a sunken teapot. They say you can retrieve a case of beer that way, too. (Huck Finn, eat your heart out.)

In 1996, the school's field trip to Vancouver was financed with the empties from the nearby Interfor logging camp, where an impressive thirty dozen beer were downed each night.

Alas, as is the case with so many coastal communities, the tiny school has since closed.

READ ISLAND

WHERE—*Discovery Islands, between Georgia and Johnstone Straits*

POPULATION—*60-ish*

CLAIM TO FAME—*Best quote ever*

If Big Bay is for big men with big wallets in big boats hunting big fish, and Refuge Cove is for J.Crew-wearing, chardonnay-sipping. yachters, nearby Read Island is where back-to-the-land hippies from the middle of nowhere go to get away from it all.

After the federal election of 2004, the Read Island results were posted on the door of the Surge Narrows general store: Greens 20, NDP 19, Liberals 7, Marxists 2, and Conservatives 1. "We still can't figure out who voted Conservative," the store owner said.

ZEBALLOS

WHERE—*40 klicks down an unpaved road off the Island Highway*

POPULATION—*125*

CLAIM TO FAME—*World's best lottery winner*

A woman once told me that as a twelve-year-old, she was urged by her father to burn down a Zeballos hotel for the insurance money. That would make him my second-favourite resident.

The first was Vinnie Parker, who was a fifty-one-year-old logger living in an eighteen-foot travel trailer when he won $1 million in the 6/49.

Reluctantly dragged in front of the media in Victoria—it was a condition of getting the cheque—he became instantly, if fleetingly, famous when he outlined his plans for the money: "I'm going to blow it."

He was going to buy some muscle cars, he said. He was going to build his own RV park so that he and his friends could party without being hassled like they were in the municipally owned one. ("Just to piss the mayor off.") He was going to get his dog laid.

"If there's anything worse than me having an attitude, it's me having the same attitude and having money," he told the *Times Colonist*'s Carla Wilson, then fled Victoria as though it were on fire, returning to the splendid isolation of Zeballos, an independent man's paradise, as fast as he could. "Let me out of here. I don't like the hassle of a city."

He proved a man of his word. Parker bought a '65 Barracuda and some other vehicles, purchased a house, got that RV park for his logging pals, bought some mini-quads for the town's kids to ride, built a great, big motorcycle track for the bigger boys to play on, and sponsored four motocross competitors. When people needed money, Parker had it, at least for six months or so. He also continued to do volunteer work around town, fixing the boardwalk, that sort of thing. (Sorry, I didn't ask about the dog, a half-wolf named Sitka.)

When Parker died at sixty-three, still a logger, he was not a wealthy man. He was, however, remembered fondly by every Vancouver Islander who ever dreamed of living large off the lottery. If you win the big one, it is their money you are spending, and therefore your moral obligation to go a wee bit nuts on their behalf.

....

OCLUCJE (pronounced OO-cloo-gee)

WHERE—*At the head of Espinosa Inlet, 12 kilometres down a perilous logging road from Zeballos*

POPULATION—*50*

CLAIM TO FAME—*Home of the last man on earth to speak Nuchatlaht*

This is true. Of the 7 billion people on earth, Alban Michael was the last to speak his mother tongue.

There's no humour in this part of the story, not when you consider how Aboriginals had their own voices drummed out of them. Maybe Native languages would have disappeared anyway, just as other minority languages have (chances are if your grandparents came to BC speaking something other than English, it didn't get passed to you), but officialdom sped the process.

Raised on Nootka Island, Alban didn't learn English until he landed at residential school in Tofino, where talking Native was banned. It was only because of his unilingual mother that he kept his Nuchatlaht. "That's how I held on to the language. I used to talk to my mother. I couldn't speak English to her."

It came in handy when he was gillnetting salmon in Nootka Sound and didn't want strangers listening when he radioed another boat. "When I wanted to keep a secret, I spoke my language." After his dad died, though, there was no one else who spoke Nuchatlaht. He could work out some of the other Nuu-chah-nulth dialects—Mowachaht, Kyuquot, Hesquiaht—in the same way a Norwegian and Swede might make themselves understood to one another, but that was it.

It's not really a rare story. By 2014, just 4 percent of BC's Aboriginal people spoke Indigenous languages fluently, according to a report done for the First Peoples' Cultural Council. Most were over age sixty-five.

The report offered a snapshot: on the west side of Vancouver Island, only 134 were fluent in any of the Nuu-chah-nulth dialects, which are so diverse that some consider them separate, and therefore more fragile, languages.

Just 165 spoke Kwak'wala, the language of the Kwakwaka'wakw on the coast and islands of northeastern Vancouver Island.

Farther south were the Salishan languages, which come from a different linguistic family altogether. Three dozen spoke K'omoks-Sliammon, while to the west, around Nitinat Lake, seven were fluent in Ditidaht. In the Victoria area, just seven were fully comfortable in the five related dialects—SENĆOŦEN, Malchosen, Lekwungen, Semiahmoo, and T'Sou-ke—found from Sooke to the tip of the Saanich Peninsula. The Cowichan Valley's Hul'q'umi'num' is one of three related Coast Salish dialects (the other two are on the Lower Mainland) that were spoken by a total of 263 people.

(Among those credited with saving the language is University of Victoria professor Tom Hukari, who was once in the US Army. One night in 1961, he was so tired that he tried to throttle another soldier who wouldn't stop playing an unplugged electric guitar.

If he had actually got his hands around Jimi Hendrix's throat, Hul'q'umi'num' might have been lost forever.)

That's it. Some vigorous language-revitalization efforts are being made, but there's no real substitute for being raised in your mother tongue. A Duncan elder told me that changing accents make it hard for today's kids to learn Hul'q'umi'num'—they speak with a hard English *k*, not the thick, back-of-the-tongue sound of their grandparents, and have trouble wrapping their mouths around the old sounds.

Alban Michael was a nice, quiet man with a good sense of humour. He laughed when I told him the last two speakers of the endangered Ayapaneco language of Mexico had had a spat and weren't talking to each other.

Alban didn't have that luxury. The others who knew Nuchatlaht were long gone.

Back in 2005, while in hospital with pneumonia, Alban had a dream in which he and his parents conversed in Nuchatlaht. Imagine that being the only place you could speak your own language.

Alban died in February 2016, quietly taking Nuchatlaht with him. In the paved, iPhoned, and Starbucked world, no one noticed at all.

A PERFECTLY

IMPERFECT CHRISTMAS

Victoria isn't great at the traditional Canadian Christmas.

We don't go for sleigh rides. We don't toboggan. We don't go carolling in the snow.

If we skate outside, it's on a rink that has more to with chemical engineering than climate. Our front yard Frosty doesn't melt, he deflates. There's a fifty-fifty chance our "turkey" is actually moulded tofu.

We might dream of a white Christmas, but if we do, we call it a nightmare—though happily for the typical Victorian, the city is more likely to feel an earthquake in the next twelve months than it is to see snow on December 25. We have endured a yuletide dusting just five times in the past seventy years, triggering the kind of panicked response that other communities reserve for pandemics, zombie uprisings, or nerve gas attacks.

What we do share with other Canadians, though, is something more meaningful, a common belief that unites us from coast to coast to coast.

That is: "Martha Stewart must die."

Okay, not *die* die. Just stop ruining the holidays.

For it was lifestyle guru Martha who, back in the 1990s, infected North America with the nonsensical notion that it is not only desirable, but possible, to have a perfect Christmas.

In Martha's world, Christmas is a Norman Rockwell painting/L.L.Bean catalogue brought to flawless life. The food is perfect. The decorations are perfect. The presents are perfectly made, perfectly chosen, perfectly wrapped.

Being perfectly selfless, Martha is willing to share how you, too, can have a perfect Christmas. Alas, try as you might, it's all but impossible to rise to the standard reached by Martha, whose website speaks of a Connecticut cottage decorated for the grandchildren, a dinner table decorated with Buri animals, pots of spikemoss to "evoke a dreamy forest floor," and an edible nativity scene fashioned by food stylist Dani Fiori.

Me, my nativity scene is edible, too, or at least the dog gave it the old college try, which is why we're down to two wise men, one of whom appears to have been mauled by a cougar. The shepherds (joined, inexplicably, by a plastic Japanese soldier) watch over a flock of headless plaster sheep (the result of a long-ago butting war) that nestle creepily around a baby Jesus who looks suspiciously like a Fisher-Price Little People character. Mary, having been drafted from another crèche with larger figurines, looms menacingly. Joseph seems to have done a runner (men are pigs).

This little scene goes nicely with (a) our misshapen Christmas tree, which appears to have been grown in the shadow of the Fukushima nuclear plant and drops needles like a drunken tailor; (b) the stockings hung with holes in their toes; and (c) the strings of lights with more burnouts than a NASCAR victory celebration.

And these mesh with the general Griswoldness of our traditional yuletide celebration: the Christmas cracker tissue crowns worn too close to the candles, the desperation gifts with the

7-Eleven receipt stamped 9:45 p.m. December 24, the boiled Brussels sprouts found stuffed down the back of the couch.

In other words, a typical Canadian Christmas.

I thought all this was good enough, but no, no, no, in Martha's world good enough isn't, well, good enough. Instead, everything must be just so.

Which is what inspired me to write my very first column for the *Times Colonist*, back in December 1997.

The impetus for the piece came on a particularly brutal winter day (I wore long pants and had to scrape the windshield with a credit card) in rural Metchosin.

It was there that I witnessed a succession of husbands and boyfriends—strong men of sturdy farming stock—brought to their knees by the unrelenting holly-wreathed hell of Vancouver Island's Christmas craft fair scene.

Understand, guys loathe craft fairs. Where women see a cornucopia of decoupage, stained glass, raku, and dried flowers, men see only Dante's Inferno with doilies. Not only that, but doilies accompanied by Sarah McLachlan's greatest hits, played on the hammer dulcimer. Yet there the men are every weekend in November and December, laden with purchases that they hold with the nose-wrinkled expression of a dog-walker rushing a plastic bag to the rubbish bin.

Why do they do this? Because it's *Hockey Night in Canada* on Saturday, and NFL football on Sunday, and they need the points. Because her last Christmas present was a vacuum cleaner, and this is penance. Because of Martha.

You see these men at the school fairs, where the surprise ingredient in the kid-made fudge turns out to be Tabasco sauce and where every craft is made from glitter, uncooked macaroni, and enough pungent glue to keep the child-artist stuck in Grade 4 for the next five years.

You see them at the church bazaars, where the No Fun Big Brother Safety Police forced vendors to stop selling the scrumptious but potentially poisonous food your grandmother used to make, yet didn't think to warn anyone that nylon yarn is flammable and should not be knitted into oven mitts.

Worst of all, you see them at the frou-frou high-end fairs, the ones that make you pay to shop, just like Costco, and where behind every table is a desperate-looking backcountry hippie whose magic mushrooms all got eaten by deer last summer and whose winter survival now depends on you buying his $700 handcrafted garden rakes. These are the fairs where you really see the guys doing the zombie shuffle—like extras from *The Walking Dead*, only more forlorn—while being pulled from table to table of folk art: wicker turkey platters, lamb-and-cat tourtière, $400 blown-glass fire pokers...

My own wife—MY OWN WIFE!—was complicit in this madness. On the pivotal day in question, she was in the Metchosin Community Hall behind a table of her handmade hats, wonderful creations that inspired delight among mothers/Audrey Hepburn wannabes and despair among the anchors they dragged.

I still recall this one miserable fellow slouching by the display while his wife spent the best part of an eternity choosing a hat for their daughter.

"I like the velveteen one," she told him.

"Then buy it," he replied, rooted about five feet behind her in the traditional bored husband position.

"But it's not reversible," she frowned.

"Then don't buy it," he replied, face clouded with the resignation of a man who had trodden this trail too many times to remember.

"But..."

That's when he keeled over like a Douglas fir—TIMBER!—crashing to the hardwood in an explosion of potpourri, lace, and tiny jars of blackberry-quinoa-compost jam, apparently rendered unconscious by the sheer tweeness of it all.

I nudged him with a toe. "You alive?"

"Go away," he hissed, still not moving. "If she thinks I'm dead, I can make a break for it."

That's when I had my dream for a craft fair beer garden, a flatbed truck that I would drive from church hall to school gym to community centre. It would have green plastic garbage cans full of bottles of Blue Buck, and chesterfields and La-Z-Boy recliners clustered around a big-screen TV featuring traditional holiday classics: *Saving Private Ryan, Slap Shot, The Longest Yard* (the original, of course). A burn barrel would double as a heat source/ barbecue for red meat. I would bring some power tools or firearms to play with. Liquor licence? Real men don't need a liquor licence.

It's also when I decided Martha had to go.

Or, at least, to back off, to stop making Christmas so hard.

For Martha, just like the rest of us, needs to accept that certain things will happen this season: Someone will either (a) refuse to, or (b) make you wear the paper crown from the Christmas cracker. Someone will accidentally burn a winning scratch-and-win ticket in the fireplace. Someone will show up at work with a sprig of mistletoe, half a gallon of Old Spice, and a roll of breath mints.

Someone will belt out a pornographic, unintentionally loud version of "Hark! The Herald Angels Sing" until silenced by a withering glare from the clergyman in the pulpit.

Someone will spend four hours in the kitchen, but be chastised for forgetting the cranberry sauce.

Someone will ask, "Do these pants make my butt look big?" to which someone else will reply, "It ain't the pants, porky," which the emergency room doctor who removes said garment will agree was unduly provocative, though this doctor will also ask that next time could you please stick with convention and just stuff a turkey instead.

Good Lord, someone will even try to make you eat Christmas cake.

When I was a boy, Christmas cakes would arrive by mail from relatives in Montreal, Portage la Prairie, North Kamloops, or somewhere equally as exotic. The groaning letter carrier would stagger up the stairs two-handing what appeared to be a paper-wrapped bar of lead, but which would, alas, turn out to be something far less edible.

For years, we would burn them in the fireplace, thinking each season's gift to be some sort of homemade Pres-to-Log fashioned from compressed sawdust. If you didn't burn it, it would just sit there like a guilty conscience. Having arrived pre-mummified, Christmas cake has the half-life of plutonium-238.

It was only out of desperation, in a year when my dad was on strike and food was scarce, that the family tried consuming one. Unfortunately, it turned out to be as dry and dense as the Criminal Code, so we went back to eating the attic insulation.

When you describe Christmas cake in this manner, its fans rush to its defence. Mostly they describe its alcohol-absorbent properties. "You should try my grandmother's recipe," they say. "It's soaked with more rum than Churchill on VE day. Two slices and you'll be climbing the tree to fight the angel."

While it's true that the best food critics do judge a dessert by its ability to get you floor-licking drunk, I'll still pass. With Christmas cake, you pretty much have to be guttered BEFORE you eat it.

But I digress.

All this reflects Christmas not as we want it to be, but how it really is, and that's just fine. We do not live in a perfect world. We do not have perfect families. We should not expect a perfect Christmas.

Accept only the ideal light display, the ideal tree, the ideal turkey, the ideal gift, or the ideal holiday, and you will inevitably be disappointed.

I think that even Martha understands this, as she reportedly treasures a clay nativity scene she sculpted during pottery class at the federal prison where she was locked up in 2004 after being convicted of ruining my life (technically, the charge was obstruction of justice). It's a wonderful piece, not only because one of the shepherds is packing a shank carved from a toothbrush (well, no, but that would be awesome), but because it proves that even Martha burns the turkey now and then, makes mistakes. This is a good thing, as she would say.

So forget *It's a Wonderful Life* and *Miracle on 34th Street*. For a classic holiday movie, watch National Lampoon's *Christmas Vacation*, which is less of a comedy than a morality play.

And have a perfectly imperfect Christmas.

GRISWOLDING, PART I

I put the Christmas lights up this week. Maybe you did, too, but when you say, "I put the lights up," it probably doesn't come out sounding like "I drank dish soap" or "I dewormed a wolverine."

Not that putting our lights up is an overly arduous task, particularly since when I say "I" did the job, it means "we," and when I say "up," it means "nothing above eye level." I no longer climb ladders at Christmas, much to the disappointment of friends and neighbours who were hoping to win $10,000 from *America's Funniest Home Videos*.

No matter how hard they try, they cannot persuade me to set the roof a-twinkle. Every once in a while, my wife will succeed in prodding me in that direction with a rolled-up insurance policy, but the effort never lasts longer than the first time a bulb busts off, leaving just the metal part buried deep in the socket. Jam a potato in it, she'll say, and I'll go, "Why don't you jam a potato in it?" and things go downhill from there. Sometimes she'll try plying me with fortified eggnog, but that just results in her husband being well lit, not the house.

This all dates back to Kamloops, in the BC Interior, and the year I was fifteen, when I climbed thirty feet up in thirty-below weather (this story gets higher and colder with each retelling) to string lights along the roof. (Hint for teens: Never tell your dad that you're bored. He has a cure.)

By the time I reached the very tippy-top, I was trembling so badly that the ladder shot out from under my boots, leaving me pedalling the air like Wile E. Coyote for what the neighbours maintain was an impressively long time. Fortunately, our house was sided with that sharp, pebbly kind of stucco, which acted as a face-brake, slowing my descent so the damage was limited to a broken nose. "Was that ever cool," exclaimed the kid next door. True story.

That was all I needed to know about decorations. I left my lights, mittens, and Christmas spirit up by the chimney where, for all I know, they remain today.

In consequence, I have not only resisted the urge to wrap today's house in new lights, but have taken to consolidating the old ones, reminding me—naturally enough—of the old 1964 Michael Caine movie *Zulu*.

Zulu was a classic big-screen epic, the kind of swashbuckler popular among those who enjoy a good old-fashioned imperialist slaughter. It was based on 1879's Battle of Rorke's Drift, in which four thousand African warriors set upon 150 British soldiers, who, as their numbers dwindled, retreated into an ever-diminishing box until they were left back to back with bayonets fixed.

My Christmas lights are the redcoats. At first, they were resplendent, marching along the eaves, down the fence and up the driveway in evenly spaced, orderly ranks. Alas, over the years the lights blinked out one by one—casualties on the ornamental battlefield—forcing the lines to contract. First they retreated from the driveway, then the big cedar tree, then had to abandon the fence.

"Too many gaps. Must consolidate the perimeter," I finally reported grimly one December day, rainwater puddling at my feet. "We have to give up the roof."

That left a tiny, brave band of bulbs clustered around the front door. It was suggested that I attempt a breakout, go to Canadian Tire for reinforcements, but I demurred. The result, which is what you see today, can be best described as "minimalist."

This is much to the amusement of my friend Darron Kloster, who laughs at my efforts in the derisive tone of the weightlifter who kicks sand in the face of the ninety-eight-pound weakling. That is because Darron puts on the most spectacular light show since the bombing of Monte Cassino. When Darron plugs in his display, the power flickers across southern Vancouver Island, and the marijuana grow-ops phone BC Hydro to complain.

How bright are his lights? Daffodils sprout and fruit trees blossom, fooled into thinking it's spring. Static crackles through the air like a snapped towel, Don King-ing the hair of passersby. A loud, electrical hum is punctuated by the occasional *pop!* of exploding pets that have been drawn to the light like moths to a flame, or Icarus to the sun. It can take months to recover the children who stumble into the forest, blinded, their retinas fried like Cheech and Chong. Darron's display is what the Second Coming would look like if they held it in Vegas.

Yet even Darron's display pales beside the record-setting effort of Australia's Richards family, whose 502,165-light spectacular, with fifty kilometres of electrical wire crammed into a single Canberra property, gained them a spot in the Guinness World Records.

Note that location. It used to be that residential displays were mostly a North American thing, growing popular in tandem with the rise of suburbia in the 1960s.

Now it's common to see homes in Britain, Europe, and even Japan lit up like Paris after the Liberation.

That's a lot of lights. A few years ago, the *Atlantic* magazine ran a story about Shijiao, China, where the world sends 20 million pounds of old Christmas lights for disposal each year. Not long ago, Shijiao metal processors would burn off the plastic and rubber to get at the copper and brass, toxic plumes of smoke rising in one of those apocalyptic eco-nightmares that make David Suzuki wake up screaming. Now they truly recycle, the insulation that wraps around the wire being recovered for the manufacture of, among other things, the soles of slippers.

And at least today's decorations are more efficient than those of the past. Old-fashioned Christmas lights were like a wildcat strike at the mill: if one went out, they all went out, and no work got done until you dealt with the dim-bulb. Today's lights use

95 percent less energy and last seven times as long. (Which, come to think of it, is my approach to work, too.)

Still, the question must be asked: Why are we so wired about Christmas lights? How did the celebration of the birth of Christ morph into a mass panic at the BC Utilities Commission? What guided the three wise men to the manger—the Richards' half-million-bulb extravaganza or a single star? The latter, of course—and if it burns out, someone else can climb up to replace it.

GRISWOLDING, PART II

I might buy the Christmas tree today. Or maybe I'll just go straight to a divorce lawyer instead.

This is an annual tradition, the hunt for the perfect—or perfectly imperfect—Christmas tree, and the trouble that follows.

Certain family members like a full, symmetrical, conical tree, lights evenly distributed, baubles spaced with a precision that would make a Swiss clockmaker cry, no ornament hung without regard to its feng shui.

Other family members think Martha Stewart should be drowned in a bucket. They prefer a Charlie Brown tree: twisted, uneven, more missing limbs than a pirate movie. Just do like you do with Granddad: hide the bald spot by turning it to the wall.

Finding the right specimen is actually much easier on Vancouver Island than in the rest of Canada, where shopping for trees is like buying a Kinder Surprise. In Real Canada they come as treesicles: frozen, trussed up, their branches lashed tightly to the trunk so that you never know what you're getting until, once thawed in your living room, they open like a flower—usually revealing something that appears to have lost an axe fight.

Not here. In Victoria, your conifer comes untrussed, its branches fully spread, allowing you to see exactly what you're buying.

As a newcomer you think this is awesome, but it's really where the problems start, where the sugar plums begin to sour.

For us, we begin our Christmas ritual by bickering so much over which tree to choose that by the time we get home, the chill in the car is colder than the air outside.

The mood doesn't improve as, with a face full of needle-sharp spruce needles, I try to blindly wrestle our tree into the house.

"Careful," she says, helpfully, as I sweep pictures from the walls and knock over lamps, scattering small children and causing slow pets to squeal.

"Language," she adds, helpfully, as I bark my shins on the coffee table. It looks as though I'm drunkenly dancing with a big green prom date, feels like I'm making out with a porcupine.

"Where am I going?" I snap, pleasantly, while randomly stabbing at the floor in search of the tree stand.

This is when we go into our Abbott and Costello "Who's on First" routine.

"Move it toward the wall."

"Which wall?"

"The one to the right."

"Whose right?"

"My right."

"How do I know where your right is? I can't see anything!"

"Don't yell at me."

"I'M NOT YELLING!" I bark, cheerfully.

"Just follow my voice," she says sweetly, opening the door to the basement stairs.

It's usually at this point that something small and furry runs out of the tree and down my leg.

Of course, whatever tree we choose will not remain vertical in the stand, a rickety device designed by the Soviet Lada factory in 1979. At best, the tree will have a twenty-degree list, as though it should be holding a martini glass. Most of the time it just keels over—*boom!*—like Mel Gibson at a traffic stop.

One year, I staggered home with a fir so big that it wouldn't fit in the stand at all. It had a butt the size of an offensive lineman's.

So I start hacking away at its trunk with an axe until it's suggested that this isn't a job best done in the living room.

Fine. I drag the tree outside, hack some more, drag it back into the house. Still won't fit in the stand.

Okay, repeat the process: outside, hack, back inside. Do this maybe four times, hauling the tree in and out like Igor looking for somewhere to dispose of the body, until she says, "Why don't you just bring the stand outside, too?"

I wish I were making this up.

By this time, the tree is naked as Les Leyne at the Times Colonist Christmas party. The carpet is covered in more needles than the Downtown Eastside. Me, I bear a striking resemblance to Jack Nicholson in *The Shining*: axe in hand, shirt askew, one eye gleaming madly and the other sealed shut with pitch.

We did eventually get the tree vertical, but only by buying a new stand whose size, stability, and price equalled that of the Mars Rover (though it was still cheaper than alimony). We pull it out every season, triggering memories that leave a warm, mellow feeling, at least until the Prozac/eggnog wears off.

My wife has suggested an alternative. She wants us to buy a live tree that comes secure in its own pot—a ready-made tree stand—ready for transplanting postholiday. It would be easy, it would be environmentally friendly, it would be stress free.

Obviously she has no sense of tradition.

Back in 2007, I attended a workplace Christmas bash that was totally lacking in inappropriate behaviour. This was, of course, a travesty; it's not a successful office party unless at least three colleagues are too shamefaced to show up for work on Monday. I wrote this as an antidote.

THE **OFFICE** PARTY

"The office party was always hazardous for anybody who thought that the key word in the term was *party*, not *office*." —Miss Manners

6:45 p.m. Right, time for the annual company Christmas bash. Pull best itchy clothes out of your closet. Reach in pocket, and find program from last year's party. Also programs from parties in 2003, 1997, and 1989. (Note to self: Are powder-blue leisure suits still fashionable?) Vow not to have more than two drinks this year. Don't want to commit career suicide.

7:30 p.m. Arrive late. Parking lot full. Four cars play musical chairs with three empty spaces. Get last spot by cutting off woman in Jaguar. Flip her the bird.

7:40 p.m. Inside, the only vacant chair is between your boss and Hank from shipping. For some reason, you and Hank have never gotten along. Decide to mend fences, make small talk: "Check out the blond babe." The blond babe must have radar, because she comes over. "Have you met my daughter?" asks Hank. Your mouth goes dry, so you down a quick Scotch.

8:15 p.m. This year's buffet menu ranges from spinach-and-pear salad to succulent roast beef and poached halibut. Superb. So superb that it's all gone by the time you grab a plate. Enjoy supper of five olives, a lettuce leaf, half a dinner roll (no butter), and a cold potato punctured by what look suspiciously like bite marks. Knock back two glasses of wine to fill void.

8:40 p.m. Boss's wife joins table. You're in her seat, but that's not why she's in a foul mood. Turns out, some idiot cut her off in the parking lot and flipped her the bird, but it's okay, she got his licence-plate number. You excuse yourself, wander outside, swap plates with Hank's car.

9:15 p.m. Lineup to bar stretches longer than the queue outside the women's washroom at a Michael Bublé concert, so you swipe a gin and tonic that someone has left on a table.

9:50 p.m. Wait to gain attention of boss. Great man. Inspirational leader. You are totally loyal to him, have been for fifteen years. You believe your loyalty will be rewarded, he has been eyeing you for promotion. Will tonight be the night? He smiles and sticks out his hand: "Hello, you must be new to the company . . ."

10:25 p.m. Turn to Hank's daughter. Would she like to dance? Yes, but not with you. Ditto for boss's wife. She's in a bad mood. Someone stole her gin and tonic, she says, staring at the glass in your hand. It is rimmed with lipstick.

10:55 p.m. You hit the dance floor and bust a few moves—as well as two chairs, an amplifier, and quite possibly the hip of old Gladys from accounts receivable. Shouldn't have had that fourth gin and tonic.

11:30 p.m. Christmas spirit/lack of food/sixth gin and tonic infuse you with mellow warmth as you sit between Hank and his daughter. Under the table, you feel her hand on your knee. You smile at her. She smiles at you. This is good. She gets up, goes to washroom. Hand is still on your knee. You look at Hank. He smiles. You down a seventh G&T.

12:15 a.m. Stagger around the dance floor, waving a palm frond snapped off a potted plant in the lobby. "How do you spell *mistletoe*?" you ask the woman from human resources.

"S-E-X-U-A-L H-A-R-A-S-S-M-E-N-T," she replies, and passes out.

12:40 a.m. You are a dancing god. The crowd can't tear its eyes from you. "Get off the table," says the boss. "You're standing on my wife's hair."

1:25 a.m. Dancing has made you thirsty. Need ninth gin. Uh-oh, wallet empty. Slip into darkened cloakroom, begin rummaging through pockets looking for cash. Good news: You find fifteen dollars in boss's wife's coat. Bad news: She's wearing it. Trip fire alarm to drown out her screaming, then run like hell.

1:30 a.m. Grab keys from table. Make hasty exit, elbowing way through throng attempting to flee "fire." Jump in car, speed off with tires and coworkers squealing. Side-swipe parked vehicles before giant Douglas fir suddenly leaps into your path. In aftermath of crash, stare at radiator steam billowing over hood ornament. Hood ornament? When did you buy a Jaguar?

HOLIDAY **HORRORS**

So, I read the first item on the list of holiday safety tips: "Make sure your Christmas tree is secure."

No problem. "You look terrific," I told the tree. "Have you been working out? You are loved, valued, and respected by your peers."

Right, on to tip two.

I've never been good with this Christmas safety stuff. Way too many "Ho-ho-hold my eggnog and watch this" moments. (Snow-covered slopes. Roaring fire. Alcohol. What could go wrong?)

Broke my nose putting up the outdoor lights when I was fifteen (see *Griswolding, PART I*). Then came not one, but two Christmas Days in Victoria General, including a visit to the ER where I became so engrossed in the brawl between the Mountie and the guy she was trying to arrest that I forgot all about the ailing infant in my arms. I even burst my appendix once to get out of spending the holidays with my in-laws.

So darn it, when the BC Children's Hospital issued advice on how to keep the kids safe this season, I put down my Scotch, pulled over to the side of the road, and paid attention.

"Every year, there are a new set of parents who may not be aware of how holiday celebrations can be hazardous to infants and toddlers," the public service announcement said.

It rhymed off a litany of holiday horrors. The glass in front of gas fireplaces can heat to four hundred degrees Fahrenheit, and take forty-five minutes to cool down. That brand-new big-screen television can squish Junior like the Wicked Witch in *The Wizard of Oz*: "More than a hundred children are brought to emergency rooms in Canada each year as a result of TV sets falling on them." Plants such as mistletoe berries, holly, and poinsettias are either poisonous or can cause irritation. (But then, the same might be said of your mother-in-law.)

The Christmas tree was portrayed as a coniferous booby trap of tasty-looking coloured lights, sharp ornaments, and easily swallowed shiny bits. To be ecumenical, BC Children's added a few Hanukkah warnings, too: "Make sure your menorah is kept on a high surface and is not too close to the edge of the table," and "Replace smaller dreidels with larger ones."

The list didn't even begin to get into the hazards posed by inappropriate toys, all those lead-based, projectile-firing, inflammable Tickle Me Trump dolls that seem like a good idea right until the newscaster uses his Tragic Story Voice to tell the tale of good gifts gone bad, a factory recall, and a class-action lawsuit.

I once bought my nephew Jake something called a Stomp Rocket, a simple apparatus linking a beer-bottle-sized missile to an air pump via a length of tubing. Stamp on the pump and the rocket would be fired high into space—or straight into your face. It wasn't until an optometrists' group declared it Worst Toy of the Year, or whatever, that I realized they called it a Stomp Rocket because Blindness in a Box might scare off buyers. Eventually the manufacturer redesigned the toy with a softer, wider warhead.

I felt bad about my purchase until I saw what Jake and his father had made: a potato cannon, a fiendish device fashioned from PVC pipe and an old barbecue starter.

It had roughly the same range and muzzle velocity as a Second World War mortar. Every time they fired it, earthquake scientists would scramble for the seismographs. Put your eye out? Heck, it would take your head off.

I'm pleased to say Jake survived both the Stomp Rocket and homemade vegetable artillery, though he still likes to tickle the feet of fate by climbing mountains and working as a whitewater-rafting guide. Oh, and a few years ago he almost killed himself (and his parents almost died from worrying) by falling out of a tree, resulting in the kind of extended hospital stay that leads people like those at BC Children's to wring their hands and fire off press releases about kids' safety, plunging televisions and poisonous poinsettias.

So happy holidays, everyone. But if you have an unsecured (or insecure) Christmas tree, better tether it to something before Jake comes to visit.

ACKNOWLEDGEMENTS

When I was a boy, my dad bought a book called *Space Age, Go Home*, a collection of pieces by Eric Nicol, the great Canadian humour columnist. I have wanted to write a book of my own ever since. It wouldn't have happened without several people whose contributions I would like to acknowledge now.

I am grateful to the people at Heritage House, including Rodger Touchie, Lara Kordic, and Leslie Kenny. Jacqui Thomas came up with a clever cover design featuring the top of my head (which I like to think of as the best half). Grace Yaginuma proved to be a meticulous, helpful editor whose criticisms were phrased much more politely than I'm used to in the newspaper world ("What would this say if you knew how to write?"). Ian Ferguson not only wrote the foreword for this book, but, along with his brother Will, encouraged me to write it.

Thanks are due to editor-in-chief Dave Obee and the rest of my colleagues at the Victoria *Times Colonist*, as well as to several other friends from the media world—Don Denton, Erin Glazier, Louise Hartland, Shannon Kowalko, Mel Rothenburger, and Kim Westad among them—who were supportive, or at least feigned interest.

Finally, I am grateful to my entire family. My wife, Lucille, who puts up with the grumpiest humour writer in Canada, deserves a medal, or perhaps a divorce.

INDEX

ABOUT THE **AUTHOR**

Jack Knox is an award-winning (but more often losing) columnist with the Victoria *Times Colonist*. Raised in the BC Interior, he
worked at newspapers in Kamloops, Regina, and Campbell River
before joining the *Times Colonist* in 1988. He served as a copy editor, city editor, editorial writer, and editorial page editor prior to
becoming a full-time columnist in 2000.

Career highlights include being blasted with blowhole spray
by Luna the whale (it tasted like fish), interviewing a porn movie
star in the nude (her, not him), and getting a phone call from
Barack Obama four days before he (Obama, not Jack) was elected
president. In his spare time Jack plays in a rock 'n' roll band with
members of his old Tour de Rock cycling team; as musicians, they
are pretty good bike riders.